WITH SCARS ON MY SOUL

A STORY OF RELEASE AND REDEMPTION

ELLEN AMY RYLES

PRESS

INTRODUCTION

"Reverend, Please Don't Go."

Rameeka walked away from the red wooden doors of the old church building with a box in her hand. It was really over. She had preached the final sermon, fellowshipped with those who had hugged her, had loved her and who had told her they didn't want her to leave. She had prayed for the congregation, asked God for any forgiveness needed, and pasted a smile on her face. If she could manage to show her big dimples it would be even better.

A lovely lady rolled her wheelchair down the side aisle that very Sunday morning followed by her daughter and son. It was Rameeka's last Sunday as the pastor of Holy Hill, and with tears in her eyes, Ada Mixon called out, "Reverend, please don't go. Don't leave me."

Rameeka's heart broke into pieces, as she looked at this lovely lady, Ada Mixon, now in the hard stages of cancer, barely able to do anything on her own. This dear woman had supported Rev. Rameeka, spoken up for her, and considered Rameeka like family since Ada's two adult children lived in Arizona. Now there was nothing Rameeka could do for the lovely Ada Mixon or for anyone else at Holy Hill Church. There was nothing Rameeka could do for anyone here anymore except pray for them. It was all over.

After worship, Rev. Rameeka Middlebrooks shook hands with the good supporters as well as the dissidents. She extended her hand and shook as firmly as any with those who had plotted, planned, lied and colluded to oust Rev. Rameeka. For some of those who had worked hard to assure her departure; it was either their conscience or their arrogance that led them to say, "I'm sorry things didn't work out, but you know we love you anyway." They were few in number and fully lacking in anything spiritual, but they were bold and shameless. Rameeka had merely looked into their eyes and said, "God bless you."

There was so much more she wanted to say. Rameeka wanted to tell the dissidents where to go, how to get there, and that indeed they were destined to get there. She wanted to tell them that their lies, their slander and their meanness were not honored by God. Rameeka thought of many things she would like to have said to the liars and the haters, but she was standing on holy ground in the Lord's house. The most professional words she could say were, "God bless you," and she knew she had to mean it. She did.

Rameeka Middlebrooks placed the box on the backseat of her friend's car and they drove away, headed to their favorite sushi restaurant in Malibu. It was time to eat well and to people-watch as she and her friend prepared to sit at their favorite table by the floor-to-ceiling window. The restaurant overlooked the Pacific Ocean, and the wind was just right on this particular day. The waves were not too rough, but just enough for Rameeka and Rochelle to enjoy the white caps on top of the waves. Later they would walk the beach, enjoy the air and give thanks to God for the ability to enjoy it.

The ladies walked into the restaurant, were greeted by their favorite hostess, and were escorted to their table. Rameeka Middlebrooks and Rochelle Mirabeau ate sushi and talked about life. These times were some of the most treasured for Rameeka. They offered respite, relaxation, laughter and hope. Just a conversation with someone she felt she could trust gave her hope and "heart health" in the theological sense. Rameeka and Rochelle had hit it off right away. As colleagues at the office who had much in common and who had lived similar life experiences, they became great colleagues and very good friends.

In spite of the strong majority of good people and those who loved and supported her, Rameeka had still been ousted from her position by a small group that had no official standing in the church. None of them held current offices or served officially during Rameeka's five-year tenure at Holy Hill Church. Some of the dissidents didn't even attend worship regularly. Rameeka reflected, as she would continue to reflect and pray about what had taken place at Holy Hill Church and why.

How had this road Rameeka traveled brought her to this place in her life? Rameeka reflected briefly on what she had come to know about the church and its need for pastoral leadership. Immediately before coming to Holy Hill Church Rameeka was a church executive in a small city in the middle of nowhere. She lived and worked in the small town she had lovingly labeled **"Nowhereland"** for seven years. The small town in New Mexico became home to her and to her daughter for those seven years. Rameeka made good friends, learned much about the history and culture of New Mexico, and learned to operate in an area that may not have offered much for African-Americans, but had welcomed her and her daughter with open arms.

So for Rameeka and her daughter, New Mexico and Nowhereland offered love and acceptance. On the other hand, Rameeka had two sons who refused to move to New Mexico. They loved Los Angeles and remained there. They shared a condo and enjoyed the ladies at every turn. Visits to Los Angeles for Rameeka and her daughter were great times of celebration; they stayed at the condo, enjoyed family time, and hung out in and around the area enjoying the company of friends and colleagues. When it was time to return to New Mexico, she would leave her sons, assure them that she was going to be all right, then Rameeka and her daughter would travel back home to New Mexico.

It might seem unlikely to some, but Rameeka had friends in that New Mexico town who would love her for life and beyond. She had been part of a community that supported her through tough times and good times. Eventually financial and political realities influenced her decision to return to a parish and to serve a congregation with a strong history and financial stability. For most African-American churches of her predominately Euro-American denomination that was a rare reality.

Rameeka's congregation was part of an independent denomination. In Southern California it was called the Southern California Area of Independent Congregations (SCAIC). As part of this Association, Holy Hill was connected to several congregations in the general area. It operated as an independent congregation connected to a district and a region of congregations that enjoyed fellowship and association with one another. The district and regional offices resourced the congregations when there was a need. Much of the work the district and regional offices did was to encourage church growth, new church plants, and healthy congregational functioning. However, the congregations were independent and wanted to remain that way. Some congregations worked more closely with the district and regional offices; others were far less connected. Rameeka's congregation was one of the congregations far less connected. She had learned the history of the separation between Holy Hill Church and the resource offices. Since learning that history Rameeka had worked to restore closer connection with some success, but not as much as she had expected. She kept connection with the district and regional staff and committee leaders. District and regional offices had a director for each office, sometimes an assistant director, and an office manager. Working to establish and maintain connection with the congrega-tions was a major focus for the offices. The connection was important as change continued to take place in the Southern California Area of Independent Congregations.

In recent years the SCAIC began to take on a different operational role with the congregations in Southern California. In Rameeka's position as a church executive she saw the change coming and the challenges that many denominations were experiencing. The reality was that many denominations were declining in membership, which meant that financial challenges were increasing. The political piece was that some regions were combining and partnering to call one regional director for two or more regions. District offices, comprising smaller areas than the region, were also combining so that executive positions were becoming fewer and farther between. Districts were calling fewer directors and assigning more responsibility. Funds were tight and positions were being eliminated. Rameeka grieved for her district and her region in New Mexico as they became more financially challenged than they had been.

Rameeka didn't want her region to be depleted of its funds; the region already had decreased to half the mem-bership of ten years earlier and had no more reserve funds. In the seven years she had served this region there had been numerous times the treasurer had to transfer funds in order to make payroll. Her region had fewer reserves to access; in other words, her region had no money. That was the reality, so Rameeka prayed about what she should do. The regional director for the areas of California, Arizona, and New Mexico was a good colleague of Rameeka. He encouraged her to consider a congregation. That meant Rameeka might be returning to the parish.

After a careful look at the reality of her position in "Nowhereland", Rameeka was approached by a congregation in Los Angeles. Accepting that call meant returning to the Los Angeles Area. Several years ago Rameeka had been pastor of King Solomon Church of Los Angeles. King Solomon Church was located in the same general area as Holy Hill Church, so she was already familiar with the community. She prayed about what God was calling her to do. Rameeka didn't want the call to be her wish, but she wanted it to be God's wish for her and the congregation. She answered the call to Holy Hill Church with a common statement, "If it is in God's plan, then yes, I will lead this congregation."

Rameeka considered the blessing in this new call and thought about the good she and Holy Hill Church could do together in the blighted community. Had this been God's call to her? She could be a pastor to her own people, and she could live back in a large urban environment that she knew. Well, that reality would certainly come crashing down.

Rameeka would continue to reflect and discern God's call after she and Rochelle had eaten all the sushi their stomachs could hold and after they had drunk enough hot sake to sink a ship. It was time to enjoy good company and think about what would come next.

A thought crossed Rameeka's mind as she and Rochelle walked into their favorite restaurant in Malibu. Rameeka wondered if the call she had answered to Holy Hill Church had been God's call. Was it God's call to Rameeka or her giving in to outside requests and consistent pressures to accept the call? Rameeka would reflect and wonder if going to Holy Hill Church was God's call to her or her call to God. The answer would come in time.

Rameeka was not above telling God what she wanted and praying that God would answer her prayers in ways that would result in what both of them wanted. Sometimes she called it "bargaining with the Lord." In the end Rameeka always prayed that God's will and God's purpose would be achieved. Her ending to prayer was, "not my will but yours, Lord. I have put what I wish before you, but in the end, Lord, it is your will that takes precedent." Part of Rameeka's ongoing spiritual journey was keeping God's plan first. Her discernment process always asked God to make the way straight.

The main issue for Rameeka was to learn and to live the lessons God intended for her to learn as she prepared herself for what was next for her ministry and for her life. As long as she learned the important lessons, harbored no bitterness toward the haters, and obeyed God's call she would discern God's answers to her questions and she would discern God's will for her life and work. God was that kind of God—always guiding and leading.

Rameeka had been quite happy as a church executive and had learned to enjoy the region in which she worked. To get to that point she had to learn how to maneuver in an area that didn't offer much for people of color, especially African-Americans. The area had history as it related to African-Americans and Rameeka learned that history. She was informed by indigenous people of all races, and she developed friends with people of every racial ethnic background in that area and beyond. Eventually "Nowhereland" became more comfortable. Rameeka had learned how deal with the cultural void, met good friends of all backgrounds and had demonstrated her leadership in and around the community. It was all good. Then she answered a call to Holy Hill, and now she was questioning whether it was really God's call or another call. How had her life come to this place in time and what would she do about it?

What had gone wrong? How had a small group of people been successful at evil? This group had formed a team hell bent on destruction. The group had no standing in the church, no official place in the life of the congregation, and no one in the group was serving on a board or a committee. So how had this small group been able to make up a pack of lies and fabrications, and be successful in rendering Rameeka to be removed from the position as Pastor? Small groups of angry members had done those things for years, and had destroyed their congregations in the process. Holy Hill was no different. A small group of disgruntled members banned together to destroy Rameeka. The only problem was that the group destroyed the church itself.

Rameeka reflected upon everything—the good times and the less than good times; then she began to review and reflect upon her life and upon her work. That's what these times were all about—prayer, meditation, reflection, how NOT to repeat errors, and how to make the future more fruitful as a result of learning lessons that had taken place. Rameeka would use her time away from Holy Hill in a productive manner.

Chapter 1

IN REFLECTION: RAMEEKA REMEMBERS

It was 4:00 a.m. Rameeka woke up from a dream in which she was in the Congo. She dreamed often and vividly, and she always paid attention to her dreams. On this particular morning Rameeka awoke to the remembrance of the rhythmic sound of drums in the nearby village from her mission visits to the Democratic Republic of the Congo. She recalled lying in her bed at the mission house where the drums made her feel like she was really "home". Somewhere in her soul she knew the rhythm, the sound, and the people. Every morning during that visit about 4:00 a.m. she awoke to hear the drums beating so that those who lived in the village could rise to the morning and prepare themselves for the day's events. During those days Rameeka would lie in bed, listen, pray and allow the rhythm from the drums to touch her soul. Then she would drift back to sleep until it was time for her to begin her day.

For about ten days Rameeka had been in the Democratic Republic of Congo, (the DRC as many referred to this country) with a small delegation. She had traveled to a slightly remote area close to Kananga where she stayed in an apartment that had been established for missionaries. She shared the apartment with a nice couple whom she had met on that trip. This couple was part of the delegation. The arrangement was quite comfortable; two bedrooms, one bath, full kitchen with a front AND back porch. Rameeka and the couple could visit with each other in the living room area, talk about their respective homes and careers and go their separate ways at other times. There was quite enough privacy and quite enough space.

They had enjoyed interacting with the people who lived nearby, who would stop by the apartment, sit with Rameeka and her friends, and learn about America. However, when asked by the Congolese officials, Rameeka did not sense God's call to missionary work in the DRC for the long term. She told the people she would consider an assignment or invitation for a few weeks to a few months, which eventually she did accept. One year following her return from the DRC, Rev. Rameeka taught at one of the Congolese seminaries for two months. Rameeka enjoyed the connection, the people, rediscovered her love for the French language, and learned some Congolese language in the process. Rameeka embraced Congolese lifestyle and culture.

The days began with breakfast from 7:00 a.m. until 8:00 am. Then they would board the bus, visit schools, hospitals and other entities to learn the history and culture of the Congolese people. Mission partnership was an essential part of the small, independent denomination to which Rameeka belonged, and she was committed to learning the good that came from that mission work while also acknowledging the other parts. She believed in realism, and no program or ministry was perfect. Her focus was how to lift up the best of the ministry and learn how to help heal the hurtful parts.

The visit to the DRC would reconnect congregations and hospitals in the general area to the denominational entity with which there was a history. The history with Rameeka's church dated back to the 1800s. The history was worth preserving, and the connection was worth renewing, especially because it involved African-American mission-aries at the helm. Rameeka had been one catalyst and one initiator.

One significant event that Rameeka referred to in her sermons told of a story on that trip when the group visited schools and churches. They were sitting on a bus and approached a newly built school in a small Congolese village. As they drove up the community welcomed them with songs, drums and the waving of palm branches. Rameeka marveled at the spiritual beauty of the people and the wonders of hospitality that transcended language bar-riers. Whereas her French was okay and helped to get her by with the people, Rameeka did not speak more than five words of the indigenous Congolese languages. However, as the only African-American female on this particular trip, Rameeka felt a strong kinship with the people. One of the Congolese women touched her shoulder while she waved her palm branch and said in English, "I know you. You have come home. Welcome home, my sister." The woman handed Rameeka the palm branch in a gesture of sisterhood and love. Rameeka graciously accepted it, simply smiled, and said, *"Merci beaucoup, ma soeur."*

Rameeka knew that the lovely woman didn't know her personally but she knew Rameeka culturally, historically, and theologically. She knew Rameeka as a woman of African descent whose ancestors had been taken away and who was returning "home" to the continent of her ancestral heritage. No matter what other racial mixture Rameeka may have claimed, the African heritage was one major racial ethnic heritage to which she proudly laid claim. Rameeka remembered that event for years to come. That trip was the trip of a lifetime.

The trip ended with a long, uneventful flight back home. For Rameeka, those were the best kind. She slept, read, watched a movie with one of her travel buddies, Philippe, and enjoyed the fact that the plane was only partially full. Rameeka and Philippe stretched across several middle seats in two different rows and rested, debriefed, laughed at the movie, and planned for the next steps in the mission. It was going to be a great mission partnership. She might even have to return to the DRC to do further work in the partnership. That would be exciting. After the President of the denomination in that area spoke with her about coming back again to teach for a month or two at the seminary, Rameeka became very excited. If she completed reading her good friend's book, she could return on a second trip to teach. This time Rameeka would teach an overview of the history of mission in the DRC. This possibility would be one of her many life goals.

Well, whatever happened, Rameeka would treasure her travels and learnings in the DRC as well her educational and mission visits to other countries throughout Africa and the world. She had also traveled to Jordan, Mexico, Europe, and South America. The continents she had not visited were on her list of things to do. Rameeka could do some of her best work in the area of understanding mission and culture, especially in the context of church growth, congregational transformation, and multiculturalism. Much of her best leadership took place there. She would remember those days fondly as she moved on to other work and other places. One plan was to look seriously at other mission visits and work in some of those other countries. She had been asked to teach in some of those places on a short-term basis like two to six months. Good possibilities as Rameeka decided how she would spend the remainder of her career.

It was now 5:00 a.m. As Rameeka reflected upon her ministry and all that she had experienced and achieved, she thought back to where she was at this place and time. How did she get to this place in her life, that is, where she was right now? She knew that God was with her in all situations, good, bad, and every place in between, but what message had God given to Rameeka from her experience at Holy Hill Church? What was God trying to tell her? She had to know and she had to really learn those lessons, because no matter where she was, God was in the mix.

And where *was* Rameeka right now? She had left her position after extreme conflict within the congregation where a small group of dissident members sought to destroy her life and her career. Now, in the aftermath of separation from the position, Rameeka meditated, reflected and prayed about the entire experience. She thought about what it meant to accept the position after a dominant male figure had been the pastor for sixty years and the kind of leadership he had exhibited. Rameeka's style was different, her manner was different and her method was different. She had brought something unique to the people.

Rameeka Middlebrooks brought international travel experience to places different than those of many members. She brought a heart for mission, education, community service and outreach. She brought experience in administration, evangelism, Christian Education, and pastoral care/counseling. She brought preaching and worship planning. She brought the wisdom to know that she could never replace the icon who had retired, nor did she want to do so.

However, Rameeka prayed that she would be able to help the church to see that its future could be shaped and informed by the past but not entrenched in it. She brought a commitment to Jesus Christ and a faith in God who could do all things. Her question for this experience was: Would the church be able to move beyond a sixty-year larger-than-life icon or would it choose to live in his memory forever? Rameeka's question for herself was: How would she heal from this devastating situation so that she would not take hurt and/or anger into the next call? Another question was: What would that next call be?

The small group of dissenters was made up primarily of women over seventy-five years of age. The group included the former pastor's wife and five sons, who didn't want to accept leadership from a female. They didn't want to have their longtime secrets uncovered either.

In addition to that, they didn't want to accept leadership from anyone who wasn't Hank Hanley. He was the icon whose sixty-year reign was now idolized by those who had loved him, hated him, feared him and who had hoped he would share the leadership. Hank didn't share. He ruled the entire kingdom, and if there were those who didn't like it or agree, he let them know that they could leave.

Before Rameeka could even begin her ministry at Holy Hill, the haters began to mobilize. Mrs. Hanley had begun telling people that she didn't believe in women pastors. She was joined in that opinion by Malina Hartman, a retired social worker who was raised in a fundamentalist home and who had been abused most of her life. She and Mrs. Hanley were close friends, and shared their disrespect for women pastors. An overwhelming majority of members voted for Rev. Rameeka; that didn't mean that the dissenters would not work at making Rameeka's experience a difficult one. At first most of the dissenters were behind the scenes. They were quiet, smiling demons with fierceness in their eyes. They would smile with their lips and look with daggers in their stares. They had a plan for Rameeka that would end in her departure.

The dissenters wanted more than Rameeka's departure. They wanted to destroy her reputation, her career, and they wanted to send her running. Soon after Rameeka began the pastoral ministry at Holy Hill she uncovered heart-breaking secrets. That was when the haters came out of hiding and rose to the forefront. Rameeka uncovered the rape of several preteen boys over many years by a seventy-two year old church officer, fistfights between members who became upset with each other, thefts of computers and other office equipment, food "disappearing" from the refrigerator of the church kitchen before and after major church events, and eight suicides within ten years. What a ministry. And why was it that Rameeka agreed to serve this church?

As in many cases and consistent with many churches, the presence of a female pastor was hard for some members, mostly other women. Rameeka had read about the difficulty some women had with female pastors. She had studied this phenomenon, talked with her colleagues, and knew that she would be aware of the reality that the church had only come so far in its progress. She wondered why the haters were so unwilling to accept her and the change that she represented. She wondered why Hank Hanley's wife Amelia was in the center of this controversy.

Rameeka had done nothing to Amelia. She had gone out of her way to be kind to Amelia, who had always been rude and nasty. Rameeka prayed about the situation, asking God to make it right and to help all of them through the tough times. Rameeka finally stopped wondering what was wrong with Amelia and decided that she, Rameeka, had done nothing. She had simply existed.

Rameeka surmised that Amelia Hanley was experiencing unresolved grief, guilt, and anger. Amelia had focused her anger with Hank, his illness, his death and his emotional abuse of Amelia upon her new pastor, Rev. Rameeka. It was easy for Amelia to join the haters because Amelia had not come to terms with many issues such as women clergy, her "lost position" as First Lady, and what her life would be like now that Hank was gone. The haters were Amelia's friends and supporters. She had loyalty issues where they were concerned. She shared her upset with the dissidents. Soon she was in the center of the controversy.

Soon the haters began to spread untruths, to scheme and to carry on in unbelievable ways. People in a congregation behave negatively when they have not grieved the death of an icon pastor in a way that leads to new life. People in a congregation do those things when they are still harboring anger toward the icon pastor about whom they now feel guilty because that icon has passed away. They make the person a god in many ways to continue covering their hurt, guilt, grief, and anger. Church people act out when they have personal issues in their lives that they cannot resolve or when they have problems they project onto others. In this case all of the above plagued Holy Hill Church where Rameeka served for five years.

Holy Hill Church still longed for Hank Hanley. Most of the members didn't know anyone else. Most of them didn't know any other way of conducting ministry or living congregational life. Hank served what was a lifetime for many; many members under sixty had never known any other pastor. He had served as pastor—-until his illnesses prevented him from being effective. That's when the church groups ran the church their way. Hank became a figurehead pastor at that point and the church didn't want anyone trying to take his place. The truth is that no one can take that person's place.

A pastor who follows an icon and who wants to lead a congregation with integrity and love would never try to replace the former pastor. The new pastor would work to encourage and engage new vision and new mission. The real truth is that no one is trying to take the departed leader's place. A new pastor accepts a position previously held by someone else and works to take the congregation to the next phase in its life. The next phase can be every bit as dynamic as the first, but times, community needs, and people change as one generation gives way to another. That was progress. Rameeka was merely trying to take the church to its next life stages. She gave her heart and soul to build upon Hank's ministry to grow the church in spirit, strength, and in numbers. The hard part was that without an interim pastor to help the church people move beyond a former pastor's reign, the congregation cannot embrace what is to come. When one continues to look to the past, the future cannot take shape or form. The past has to be reckoned with in order to face and embrace the future.

Rameeka continued to build the ministry at the church as best she could in healthy ways. She was trained in leadership development, church conflict management, methods in congregational health and congregational transformation/church growth. In this work at Holy Hill Church, Rameeka Middlebrooks had come up against conflict, jealousy, desire to claim and reclaim power, and cowardice in ways that she never knew existed. From all of the gossip, inaccurate information, and anonymous letters that her former members wrote, the ministry was difficult from the beginning. Difficult from beginning to end. Now after five years it had ended. How and why? And where would Rameeka go from here?

Even beyond where Rameeka would go, what would the large number of supportive members do after her last Sunday? Many of the strong leaders who had been active in the church and community as well as those who were strong financial supporters declared that they would not return to Holy Hill Church. The dissenters had already declared that those who threatened to leave would return so the detractors were not concerned at that time. Their main focus was to get rid of Rameeka and to gain or regain control of Holy Hill.

Eventually the conflict would take its toll on the congregation and even on the community in which Holy Hill was located. The deep unrest had already taken its toll on Rameeka. She was leaving with no position to follow. Even though she had a one-year severance package, she could not take it easy. She had to keep seeking. She would definitely keep searching, but in the meantime she would vow to take better care of her body, mind and soul. Rameeka went home to release herself of the immediate pressure by taking a long walk, reflect upon nature and God's handiwork in the world, and then find redemption in whatever God would provide for her next position.

Chapter 2

SWEAT AND BLOOD

A s usual Rameeka awakened about 4:00 a.m. She looked into the darkness of her bedroom where the filtered light from the streetlamps peeked from in between the blinds. She lay in her bed and prayed. Sometimes prayer was difficult when she thought about her current circumstances. In those cases Rameeka would just pray the Lord's Prayer and ask God for grace and mercy. Somehow she was still able to beseech God's care. She knew she would get through the situation but the raw pain of the "right now" had a hold of her heart. She lay in the still darkness and repeated the prayer she knew best.

"Our Father, who art in heaven, hallowed be thy name. Thy kingdom come, Thy will be done on earth as it is in heaven. Give us this day our daily bread and forgive us our debts as we forgive our debtors. And lead us not into temptation, but deliver us from evil. For thine is the kingdom, and the power and the glory, forever and ever. AMEN." It was after this prayer her mother taught her from the earliest days of her memory that she could move into her own personal plea to God.

"Gracious and Almighty God. I come to you as your child created in your image, called to do your work according to your will. Touch my soul, cleanse me of all unrighteousness, and grant in me a clean heart to serve you with the best of everything you have given me. Lord, you know what I tried to do and that I tried to be as faithful as I could be. You know what I tried to stand for. You know my heart, and you know that any errors I made were done in good faith, trying to serve you with the best of everything I have. Whatever I may have done to contribute to this current situation, Lord, forgive me. Allow me to use this time to be drawn closer to you and to trust you in every way. Restore me to the joy of your salvation, and let me serve you in spirit and in truth. Move me through the situation now, Lord, and use me to and for your purposes. In Jesus's name I pray. AMEN."

Now, at least for the moment, Rameeka could rest. She allowed the sounds of the night to lull her to sleep. For the next three hours she could find peace.

Chapter 3

A GOD SOMEWHERE

Rameeka walked her daughter's dog the next morning and allowed the little rascal to walk all over creation. Sometimes Fritzie liked to take his time walking. He was a small dog, Shitzu and Maltese mix, with all the personality of such breeds. Fritzie was a barky little character, nervous, and always trying to let the world know how tough he was. Large dogs just looked at him, and made no move until Fritzie would allow the rest of his reactions to really reflect the constant wagging of his tail. He would finally stop barking, touch noses with the other dogs, and then each dog would "examine" the other. Finally they could be friends. Fritzie had lots of friends, and his best friends were fellow Shitzu's in the neighborhood. Rameeka and her neighbors lovingly called their Shitzu's and Fritzie "cousins".

This morning walk was one representing her prayerful state of mind these days, and provided a peaceful way to begin the day. Rameeka saw the beauty of the morning, felt the warmth of the sun, and embraced the hope that had to lay ahead for her. Certainly the Lord vindicated the Lord's people, right? Surely the Lord would fight Rameeka's battles and render her free to serve another congregation or another district or region, right? Wasn't there a God somewhere?

Rameeka always believed there was a God somewhere beyond the sky, in her soul, all around her, and now was the time to call upon that God. Rameeka called upon God for all she was worth as she walked yet another hill with Fritzie. She called upon the Lord to set things right, and to move her to the next step. God would undoubtedly move in God's time, it was just that God's time wasn't always (or sometimes ever) human time. There was an old phrase, "The Lord may not come when you want, but the Lord is always right on time." Rev. Middlebrooks wanted that time to be now.

Well, at least in twelve months Rameeka wanted that time to come because her severance would run out. "Lord," she prayed, "Please make your time come to fruition within a year, 'cuz I'm going to need a good position that pays what I make now or more. Take care of your child, Lord. AMEN." In the meantime, Rameeka's sweat from the morning workout with Fritzie created symbolic and theological great "drops of blood" from the Gospel of Luke as she and her "grand dog" walked the path from the road to her front door. It was only 7:00 a.m., and this one hour of the day had been spent in movement with God.

Chapter 4

WHAT IS REQUIRED OF US?

The pressure of what was required of a pastor who had been forced out of her congregation mounted. How nice it would have been if Rameeka could have been completely done with Holy Hill Church. However, there was one more step in the final farewell. That last step was an appreciation celebration. The thought process in a congregation providing such an event had to do with closure and finality. The final reception/dinner/event was designed to say goodbye to the pastor no matter what circumstances prevailed, and for the congregation to be able to close one chapter before embarking upon another.

Rameeka resigned herself to the reality that she had to be the guest of honor at a special dinner held to show appreciation for her service with Holy Hill Church. She never appreciated final farewells when someone's call didn't end peacefully. They always seemed so phony. All who were present had to smile, say nice things, pretend that they loved each other when often that wasn't true at all. Those farewell events were designed to bring closure to that chapter of the call. They usually created even more pain and headache than just leaving things the way they were.

Rameeka's call had ended in disaster with a small, hateful group of people who had printed lying brochures of slanderous foolishness about her and had sent them all over the community. The mean little group had contacted their friends and family around the country, trashing Rameeka and slandering her in so many ways, even slandering her on an Internet social network. Now she had to attend a farewell event and pretend that everything was all right. How phony was that?

Arriving a bit early, Rameeka opened the door to the building. She wondered if any of the haters would be in attendance. She hoped the hell not! Of course those who planned the dinner had arranged it so that none of the haters could be present. At the time Rameeka didn't know that, so she was a little concerned and on edge. Well, one person who had never realized that there were times he had been a thorn was present. Rameeka looked at her former member and smiled. Oh brother! Smiling in the face of failure, being gracious in the reality of what was gone, and holding up under hostility sat like a big rock in the pit of Rameeka's stomach. She took deep breaths as she walked into the front door of the beautiful facility in which her farewell celebration was being held.

She eyeballed the reception area, and saw who was milling around. God had been gracious. Rameeka saw only friendly faces. She saw only supportive people—those who had stood behind her and held her up during her few years at Holy Hill Church. Chilled champagne mimosas greeted her at the table along with unlimited hugs from well-wishers. Rameeka allowed Captain Aaron Arnold to hug her as the military officer stepped from around the table to show his former pastor the respect he had always intended to show. In Rameeka's mind that intent didn't always transfer into real support or real leadership. Captain Arnold was caught between the detractors and the supporters. Riding the fence in this case meant that Rameeka had written him off and just continued to show respect and civility. That was the best the Rev. could do in this case. One could not ride the fence in the Lord's work.

The Captain and his wife, who was a Colonel, retired from twenty years of military service, and had settled back in Los Angeles, their home city. Captain Arnold had enjoyed the benefits of being married to a Colonel and the status it brought. Of course he had achieved much in his own right. However, not ever having been in leadership as a church officer had its challenges for the Captain. Well, the Captain felt that he had supported Rameeka and would have been saddened to know that many of his suggestions and recommendations had been anything but supportive. Rameeka reflected momentarily over the blunders the Captain had made, some of which resulted in a mess for the church. Rameeka just spoke kindly and walked to the next well-wisher.

She stepped inside the banquet hall; saw that more than one hundred fifty people who loved her were gathered together. Now she could some spend time with them. When it was time for the official beginning of the banquet, the former chair of her search committee prepared to escort her into the celebration. He and his lovely wife Sylvia had been her lifeline during the good times and the hard times. Rameeka loved this couple who had become her Pasadena sister and brother. They had welcomed her into their home, provided a solace and a refuge from the highest heights of the conflict at Holy Hill, and had expressed their complete dismay at the fall out. She would keep them in prayer.

Rameeka took a side step to the mimosa table for another quick sip as she prepared to enter the banquet hall. The caterer winked at Rameeka as she lifted the second mimosa glass to her lips. That woman knew what Rameeka enjoyed at social gatherings. There was nothing like a really good champagne mimosa at a fancy event. Well, the second mimosa hit the spot just before she took that final walk. For Rameeka, even though she was very familiar with this beautiful crowd, she always got butterflies in her stomach just before preaching or leading a public affair. Today was no different. She would be expected to respond publically to the ceremony; she thought carefully about what she would say as she prayed for God to calm the butterflies. God was truly at work on this lovely day.

Chapter 5

HOLY HILL VERSUS HOLY COMMUNION

The farewell dinner had gone very well. The music was extraordinary, and the leaders had gone all out for this day. It touched Rameeka's heart and even brought forth a few tears from her own eyes. This group had treated Rameeka very well, and had supported her through the wind and the rain, and through the storm and the fire. There was always a faithful group that wanted progress and a future.

This group loved Rameeka, called her into account-ability, was direct and honest with her, and stood by her. They were open minded, sincere, and forgiving. Representing more than eighty percent of the entire con-gregation, this was the group of strong leaders, officers and supporters. They were the movers and shakers. They were the committed financial givers and the real go-getters. After the tragedies, the conflict, and the fallout they were at this function for Rameeka. So many of them vowed that they were not going back to the church where Rameeka had been ousted. What a loss that would be! All the strong, ethical leaders were leaving the church where they had been members and officers for several years. Rameeka had no control over who would return to Holy Hill and who would not, but on this day she appreciated their love and respect for her.

Holy Hill Church was located in Compton, California in a residential area not far from King Solomon Church where Rameeka had previously served. The neighborhood showed all the signs of blighted, inner-city scars. Boarded up homes, others in need of repair and renovation, and still others were occupied by many families that were barely making it from one moment to another. So much could be done; so much needed to be done, and Rameeka had begun to make some inroads with the community and civic leaders.

For five years she had given her soul to the families of the congregation and the community. For five years she had buried their dead, baptized their babies, married their children, and taught Bible study. She had provided pastoral care, listened to their difficulties, and been there for them in all situations. She had accompanied the wayward to court, testified to the willingness of others to lead a new life, and welcomed new members.

She had shared dreams and hopes. She had met with community leaders, businesspeople, the governing board of the church and many others on numerous occasions. She had written proposals and obtained grants for special programming. She had worked hard to move the church forward. Rameeka had served on church, civic, community committees and task forces. She had cared for all of the people whether they were community residents, community leaders, church members, or folk who were just passing through. That was what God required. She loved all of the people; they were her people—all of them. Some of them just couldn't allow Hank Hanley to rest in peace. They wanted to resurrect him. They tried hard to do so.

It seemed that Holy Hill would take a few steps forward then something would take them back. Of course the most devastating event was the child sexual predator. That situation devastated everyone even after he was imprisoned. The child predator plead guilty to thirty-six counts of child sexual abuse, sodomy, having sex with a minor in a public place, rape, forcible rape, and other multiple counts. He was where he belonged. The heartbreaking part was that several older women lifted up the child rapist as a hero who had been done an injustice. Go figure.

Then there was the seventy-eight-year-old usher who sexually harassed women as they came to worship; there was the disturbed woman who was accused behind the scenes of incest with her sons AND daughters. There was the father who had raised his daughters and had been quietly lifted up as the one who had molested each of them. Embarrassing tragedies. Human sinfulness. Mental illness at work in the life of the church and in the world. Following her handling of these situations in the appropriate manner, the little old ladies blamed Rameeka. In their minds Rameeka had put the rapist in prison and

Rameeka had removed the old Casanova from the usher board. Well, she knew she would be the one blamed if anyone was. Rameeka could handle the backlash and the pushback. She had taken the correct action according to the law and to the church. She had been advised by legal counsel from the national office, the district and regional policy directors. Also, Rameeka had contacted and maintained communication with those authorities at each step of the process. Rameeka had done the right thing. She had done what God had led her to do after learning about the abuse of a young woman who was a minor at the time. She wasn't responsible for "getting someone convicted". The truth was that we are responsible for our behavior, and we experience the consequences of it. Sometimes when one does the right thing, resistance forces the opposite results to occur. For a congregation that had been steeped and entrenched in hidden secrets and shame, it was no surprise that the congregation's hurt and anger had risen to the surface. Rameeka reflected upon the situations many times and came to one conclusion. Where it involved the rape of children, the sexual harassment of certain people, and the unresolved issues of suicide, Rameeka would do it all again.

That didn't mean Rameeka hadn't made some mistakes of her own. She had moved the folk faster than she might have. She had grand ideas and could have been more patient in implementing them. A congregation in which more than seventy percent were over seventy-five years was a congregation that couldn't change easily. Rameeka should have thought about that harder. She had listened to the progressive group without questioning some of their opinions and without checking things out as closely as she might have with several other members who might not have been as progressive. Her advisory team consisted of the search committee and some members of the church board who had served faithfully. They loved Rameeka and wanted to see the church progress; it was just that the push to move progressively could have been done a bit more slowly. Balance is key in these situations, and Rameeka thought she had a balance. Next time around she would take more time to learn the people and the history; some things required serious action; some things required time and study.

Rameeka reflected upon her dear friend and brother in the Spirit who had come to Holy Hill to provide leadership and energy. Renaldo Timmons, a pastor from Phoenix, Arizona, had known Rameeka since she was far less experienced. For fifteen years Renaldo had been a trusted pastor and mentor to many. He preached a week-long revival at Holy Hill; he led the congregation in an educational learning experience on change. Renaldo talked about the need to implement change slowly like a captain turning a cruise ship. His key word—"slowly".

Rameeka could have taken some issues more slowly. One was Holy Communion. Certain folk were not ready for the change in Holy Communion after sixty years.

Some didn't like the new method while others welcomed it. The entrenched folk who didn't want change didn't like the choice in Holy Communion. They had never known about Intinction, the practice in which a person takes a piece of bread dips it gently into a common cup of wine and partakes of the bread and wine together. What they didn't know, they didn't like. It was as simple as that.

Rameeka had intended to encourage the church to participate in Intinction once in a while. However, the advisory team knew about Intinction from their participation and leadership in the wider church and through other denominations. They asked for it regularly. Thinking this group represented the majority Rameeka agreed and asked the governing board to approve the choice of traditional and Intinction so the congregation would have a choice. That approval was unanimous. Well, some of the folk were locked into the practice of having the officers come to serve them. Also they were locked into the flat wafers, not real bread. So Wesley Winkle, a member of the Church Board, went outside of the Board to complain about the new-fangled Holy Communion practice. He sought out several members and gossiped with them. He was a piece of work, that Wesley Winkle, a quiet retired grocery store owner who chose to go outside the Board instead of just talking with the pastor as several had advised him. He wasn't accustomed to women in leadership and never approached Rameeka. Rameeka never trusted him after that and always kept him at arm's length. Good choice.

Rameeka reflected on the fact that she should have put that change off for a year or so. Maybe that would have made a difference, and maybe not. The other changes were truly needed. They involved policy, finance, governance and visioning. When a pastor walks into a church in which interim work should have been done and was not, then usually that pastor becomes the one who leads the interim work. Rameeka was what the church unofficially labeled an "unintentional" interim. That meant that she was the pastor who actually led the congregation through the transition period because it did not occur for whatever reason. Even though she was not the official interim, Rameeka became the Interim Pastor. Whether it was two years or five years, she was the Interim Pastor.

Holy Hill Church had not been assigned an interim, which was devastating for everyone. Some of the Holy Hill Church leaders felt that this particular African-American church would not benefit from the usual practice of having an interim. Their argument was that the church had been accustomed to long-term leadership and would not fare well with an interim for two years. Unfortunately for everyone, it seemed that the district office and the regional office took this group seriously. Having been a church executive herself, Rameeka knew a game when a church played one. She had experienced congregations of all types who had attempted the same tactic. Rameeka was not in favor of such practices and did not allow congregations to get away with those practices. She followed strict rules in these cases. Sometimes the congregation was successful in convincing a regional body that an interim was not needed, and the church would be allowed to skip a crucial step. That was not a good idea because it meant eventually that everyone would suffer the consequences. Such was the case with Holy Hill.

There was another crucial step that was left alone. The regional office had not advised or insisted that the Hanley Family take its leave of the church and the community following Hank's retirement. He and the family remained until Hank died 18 months after Rameeka arrived. The district and regional offices, special committee, and community leaders felt that Hank would not be a threat since his illnesses had taken over and he was unable to function. What a fatal mistake. The regional office and the particular committee responsible had not figured in "First Lady" Amelia and her five children. These entities had not figured on a small group of detractors who would seek to destroy any pastor who followed Hank. Their frustration was directed at Rameeka or whoever may have been serving the congregation, but the real issues were deep below the surface. Many of the issues had nothing to do with Rameeka.

In so many ways, white systems did not know or understand African-American culture or traditions. They thought they knew, especially those Euro American people who had significant contact with African-Americans and other people of color. They thought they knew the people. They never would. Rameeka had performed many interim duties at Holy Hill. She had officiated at the funeral for Hank. She had given him a royal "homegoing". Unfortunately Amelia and three of her five children remained at the church where their anger and inappropriate grief turned into a power battle against Rameeka. A few others had joined them and made Rameeka's tenure a battle for power. How unnecessary. What they didn't know was that Rameeka didn't enter power battles; she just continued to be the pastor and head of staff. Those power struggles were part of the reality when a congregation had not been assigned an interim.

What some congregations do not understand is that the interim process is designed to help a congregation such as Holy Hill Church to grieve the loss or departure of a pastor, particularly one who has served long-term. The interim process allows a pastor to serve the congregation and to assist the congregation in its preparation for future leadership. When an interim serves a congregation, usu-ally for a period of between one and two years, that person prepares the congregation for the next pastor whom it is hoped will serve for several years. The interim pastor has specialized training, works closely with the church lead-ership to reshape and revision the congregation's focus on ministry and its vision. During this time, the former pastor and his/her family are expected to leave the congregation to help prepare for new leadership.

Many denominations follow the practice that insists that a retiring pastor and his or her family take leave of the congregation and in some cases, the community. The reason is very simple: it is essential to prepare a congregation for new pastoral presence. This practice, the practice of interim leadership and the retiring pastor and family to take leave, allows new leadership to enter the congregation with more of a chance to be successful.

When a long term pastor or any pastor retired, resigned, died, or departed for any reason, the special pastor, the intentional interim pastor was assigned for up to two years. The interim pastor accepted the role to help the congregation through a period needed to prepare itself spiritually and emotionally for a new installed or "permanent" pastor. The "unintentional" interim was usually a pastor who followed a long time pastor and experienced difficulty. In those situations experiences occurred because the congregation thought it was ready for new leadership, when actually it was not ready at all. In reality there was much more work to do.

The grief, anger, guilt, and hidden secrets had not been revealed prior to Rameeka's entrée. Therefore, Rameeka would be the pastor who would lead the congregation through that transition. A congregation that had not experienced a healthy transition period or a healthy grief period often projected its frustration onto the next pastor. The congregation might take its frustration out on a pastor like Rameeka without realizing what it was doing.

In Rameeka's case a small group of people had resisted change and had never grieved properly for the illness and death of Hank.

This small group had been angry at the arrest and imprisonment of Aaron Morrow the child rapist, had been angry at the agreed upon removal of Lavon Jackson from the usher board at the accusation of sexual harassment, had ignored the need for updated bylaws after ignoring thirty-five-year-old bylaws that had never been revised. The congregation also denied the importance of personnel policies that had not been revised in thirty years. In addition to the old bylaws and misconduct, the congregation overlooked suicides, played down the fist-fights, and scoffed at the lack of concern about security and who had access to the church building. Rameeka had dealt with all of these issues appropriately and through correct channels. The fall out had been insurmountable over the five years.

A pastor like Rameeka would complete the transition/interim work and realize that she could not remain with the congregation for the longer term. However, she had done much of the work that was needed for transition so that the congregation could call a new pastor who might be successful if the dissidents didn't move the church all the way back five years. Well, Rameeka had done the work in the best way she knew how. Now another "intentional" Interim pastor would come and spend two years redoing what she had led the congregation to do during her five years. That was no longer her concern. Rameeka took the time to enjoy her Sunday afternoon with the people who showered her with love, accolades, gifts and hugs. She was truly appreciated. Rameeka left the farewell banquet and drove to her friends' home for more celebration and good conversation. It was going to be a long but enjoyable day!

Chapter 6

RAMEEKA-ON THE REAL!

R ev. Rameeka woke at 3:00 a.m. and meditated for at least an hour before she realized that she needed to get up and begin her day. She would awaken very early during her time at Holy Hill Church. There was always something for which to pray, to beseech God, and for which to prepare. She had risen many mornings at 3 or 4 a.m. to write grants for funding or to prepare for Bible Study. Her best times for creative thinking and preparation were between 3 and 6 a.m. Likewise her best times for the Spirit to move within and upon her, and for dreams to be most memorable, were those same times. Interesting how God worked.

Rameeka prepared thank you notes to those who had provided such a fine celebration. It had taken her longer than she had intended, but she prayed the people would understand. While she sat at her desk writing and remembering the lovely dinner and the music, Rameeka sat back for a moment to think about her journey to Pasadena and Los Angeles, and how God had brought her to this place and to this time.

It had been quite a life journey from Chicago, Illinois to Princeton, NJ to Rancho Cucamonga, CA, New Mexico, Pasadena and Los Angeles. What might it have been like if she had remained in Chicago all of her life? She had been born and raised there, and even though she had traveled around visiting family, had seen much of the U.S. and Europe, especially Paris, by the time she was nineteen, she wondered what life might have been like if she had continued to live her entire life in Chicago.

Somehow learning about her mother's travels as a young woman, her father's journey as a WWII veteran, how France and other countries were open and welcoming to African-Americans, particularly soldiers, were exciting to Rameeka. She loved listening to their stories and seeing pictures from those days. Some of the desire for a life journey in travel extended to her brother, Bobby, and his enjoyment of Paris and other parts of France during his time in the Army; these realities grabbed ahold of Rameeka's heart. She took French in junior high, high school, and college. The language served her well when she traveled to Paris, Nice, and the Loire Valley with her professor, his wife and about fourteen other classmates during college. What an experience. She learned that many European men were openly attracted to women of African descent, and vice versa, seemingly without so much of the open repercussions of such relationships in the United States. These couples walked the boulevard, lived together, raised families, and enjoyed life. In Chicago during her high school and college years, people still stared and whispered.

Rameeka learned that some African-American writers and musicians made Paris their home. At one point in life Rameeka wanted to do that, make Paris her home. It was her favorite city in the world, no doubt because it was the first city in Europe in which she had actually lived. Yes, she had been to Niagara Falls, Canada, and Windsor, Ontario, but they were just across the bridge from Buffalo and Detroit—but Paris! It was way across the Atlantic and had been home to so many of her favorite artists, writers, and performers.

Of course Rameeka would not stop at just living in Paris for herself. She would have wanted to bring her entire family to Paris, something they would never do. She learned that the world was far wider and broader than her little space in it. She developed a love for international education and for the people of the lands. Paris became even more of a city of celebration and delight when she visited Paris a second time with her sister and her daughter. That visit was when she really learned the city. They walked the city together in the rain, in the slight fog, and all weekend. What a joyful visit. Rameeka's beloved niece had treated her and her sister to a trip to Europe to visit while Rameeka's daughter was living in Germany. Thanks Di!

One of her greatest moments of true sisterhood back in the day was when she was blessed to meet Rhamissa in Paris. She was taking pictures during a break from classes in Paris, and saw a lovely woman of African descent standing nearby. She took advantage of a moment and asked a young woman if she could take her picture. The African woman smiled and said she was honored. Then her classmates joined in and all of them became friends, posing, laughing and getting to know each other. They went for coke after the pictures, and Rhemmett told Rameeka she was from Ethiopia, living and studying at the Sorbonne.

After that day, Rameeka and Rhamissa were sisters in the Spirit. They spoke by phone from time to time during Rameeka's tenure in Paris. When Rameeka returned to the States after classes were over, she and Rhamissa wrote to each other for a good while.

They lost contact until Rameeka served her first congregation as an Associate Pastor in Rancho Cucamonga. There she met a Black French family. Believe it or not the family knew Rhamissa, who was now married with a family of her own and still living in Paris. How small the world was! Yes, the international world took hold of Rameeka's soul and she loved meeting and making friends with people everywhere. So what message was God was trying to instill into Rameeka's heart and soul? And why was she following her brother's footsteps to California, her Dad to France, and her Mom to all the states around the South, especially Florida and St. Simon's Island? Oh yeah, and why had she married a pastor herself like her only sister had done? What was she seeking and who was she imitating?

Of course her family had gone to these places when they were young and single. Rameeka drug her three children all around the country while she was in seminary, practicing ministry, and still talking about settling down, remarrying at some point, and living a nice mundane, routine life. Yeah, right!

Either it wasn't in the cards or Rameeka would be an eternal opportunist, taking good advantage of situations in which she could be in ministry. Her children had sort of enjoyed the moves—sometimes! It was hard on them, but what choice did they have? They loved their Mom, and at the time they were minors. The children were not blind to her faults, but they knew she did the best she could to take care of them and to provide for them. They knew that whatever she had was theirs, and whatever they needed she would make every attempt to obtain. Rameeka's children were her life back then when they were young teens and certainly now as young adults. She loved them from the soul and would be there for them in any and every way she could. They were very close as a family and tolerant of each other's imperfections. Rameeka admitted that she had many imperfections. One of her beloved mentors always taught, "All imperfections are made right in the resurrection." Rameeka believe that statement, especially now.

This morning as Rameeka penned thank you notes and prepared them for mailing she realized once again that she was a middle aged pastor without a church or regional office to run, sitting in her townhome with a broken heart. She remembered a book she had read about the Lord who mends hearts that were torn apart and heals shattered spirits. The Lord God puts us back together when we fall apart. This was the God Rameeka knew and trusted; this God would work on her behalf. What a fine theologian the author was. The book had ministered to her soul in profound ways. It gave her hope and renewed her spirit.

Rameeka prayed for the congregation she had just left. She prayed for the small group of dissenters who had been so cruel and had lied so vehemently. She prayed for the group that had left the church, vowing never to return. Rev. Middlebrooks didn't know if they would return, for they were dealing with pain and spiritual suffering. They were in a spiritual diaspora, this faithful group who loved Rev. Rameeka Middlebrooks. They entered a physical diaspora as it related to a home congregation. All Rameeka could do was pray for them. Rameeka prayed for the world that God had created, asking God to restore the entire cosmos to what God had intended upon creation. That was one of her regular prayers. She prayed for her family, for the world, for safety and salvation for children, for the elderly, as well as for those who suffered from disease, illness, and homelessness. Finally, she prayed for herself.

"Lord", she prayed, "Heal my broken heart, restore me to the joy of your salvation, help me to forgive those who have lied about me, and forgive me for anything I may have done wrong. Grant to me a ministry you lead, ordain, and provide in the Name of Jesus Christ our Savior, AMEN."

Rameeka opened her eyes from prayer. It was 8:00 a.m. She took a deep breath and went back to bed. The next three hours belonged to dreamland.

Chapter 7

LET DIVINE ORDER RULE

The 110 Freeway was always crowded. If that wasn't bad enough, the 10 and the 405 always seemed to invite accidents and delays. Rameeka had learned to leave home at least an hour before any scheduled meeting in order to arrive on time. While it always seemed like a waste of time, it was always the right thing to do. When she was the pastor of King Solomon Church she would leave home at 7:30 a.m., just in time to listen to AM radio, hear the spirited AMEZ pastor followed by the Baptist pastor. What a way to bring spirit to her preparation for Sunday morning worship!

Their prayers and preaching put her on a spiritual high. She would drive the 110 shouting "Hallelujah!" She would do so in a refined and classy manner of course. Upon arrival to King Solomon Church, Rameeka would be in a spiritual place to lead worship with zest and excitement for a fine group of people in and around Compton and Gardena. She would drive the 110 to Rosecrans, make a left and drive straight to the church, crossing Figueroa, Main, San Pedro, Avalon, and Central. She knew the ride very well—every shop, restaurant, store, and vacant lot. She would always arrive by 8:15 a.m., which was a little more than two hours before worship. What a time for prayer and meditation, review of her sermon, and good gospel music in the background. These mornings provided ministry for the soul. God had smiled on Southern California.

Rameeka left King Solomon Church with sadness and joy at the same time. She had learned of a position at the national office and thought it might be a good way to serve the Lord and to make a good career move as a church executive. She had always loved the idea of traveling and serving the world in a broader manner. But there was one huge question. Was this what GOD wanted? Rameeka knew that it was what she wanted, but what did the Creator have to say about it? And what about that fine police lieutenant who had been courting her for a year? He was talking about settling down with her, becoming married, and enjoying life together. Where was their relationship headed now, and how dead in the water would it be when she moved to back to her hometown of Chicago? After all, this man was a native of Los Angeles, and it seemed that most people from Los Angeles didn't do long distance relationships well, or at all.

There had been so much to decide upon back then. Rameeka prayed so fervently in those days she didn't know how to open her eyes without her staple prayer to begin the day. Her prayer partner the Bishop had shared that prayer with her several years ago, and it became her standard start for the day. "Loving God, let your Divine Order rule my day and my decisions. Keep the world in your eternal care. AMEN."

With that prayer and the research she had done, Rameeka accepted the executive position and took off to the national office and to back to Chicago. It had been quite an adventure. God had prevailed, as always, and Rameeka had been the better for it. When time was right and God showed the way, Rameeka returned to her adopted home in Los Angeles. It felt like God had been gracious, knowing that LA was in her soul. That was where God knew Rameeka could minister best and most effectively. For Rameeka, that was Divine Order and God's plan. Yes, Los Angeles was where she belonged.

Chapter 8

SUSHI AND SAKE

In the restaurant with Rochelle, the sushi and sake had taken their effect so that the friends smiled at their meal, conversation, and newfound freedom. Rameeka sat back with her best friend and talked about how much they needed that respite. Rochelle agreed. All that sushi, sake and laughter resulted in a positive feel to the afternoon. The two sisters in the spirit talked about their newly acquired status of being unemployed. Rochelle was already retired and could have left upon Rameeka's entrée to the church five years earlier. However, Rochelle had continued working to support Rameeka as a new pastor, helping her to learn the ropes of a new call.

Rameeka had a few more years to go. She sat back for a moment of silent thought. She had some planning to do and another position to acquire for at least fifteen more years. Then she could retire and return to her once beloved home of Virginia Beach, VA. She and her children owned a townhome there. Once they had owned three. The economy in a few years past had made it necessary to rid themselves of two. The kept the first one. That was where she thought that she would return one day unless God intended for her to retire in Los Angeles.

Rochelle sat back after she had finished her last sip of hot sake. She felt the bonds of sisterhood with Rameeka. Rochelle saw Rameeka was a rookie when it came to African-American churches and communities. Rameeka had worked and lived away from them for so long that Rochelle wondered if Rameeka could really relate on one level. On another level Rameeka was sincere and committed to making life better for those who were still trapped in the inner city. She wanted to give the young people a start and the older ones the security of knowing that they were loved and that the Church was a place of love, service and faithful commitment. Yes, Rameeka had needed a little help understanding this particular community and congregation. It was not like those Rameeka had served before.

Rochelle was loyal and committed, and she fought for as good a pastoral experience as she could provide for her new parson. She had liked Pastor Rameeka immediately, and often said that she was committed to "retiring" a second time but then she got to know Rameeka. Rameeka was likable and easy to get to know. She had been a kind supervisor, and was willing to listen even if she didn't follow all of Rochelle's advice. Not listening to Rochelle had gotten Pastor Rameeka into hot water a few times. In those cases Rochelle would step in and smooth things out, realizing that Rameeka had not meant to ignore her, but had just listened to the wrong folk. Church politics was something Rochelle knew well, and she never minded straightening things out behind the scenes.

Rochelle served Holy Hill Church for fifty years, since about ten years after Pastor Hanley had arrived there. She knew all his secrets and all his faults. Rochelle knew just about everything there was to know about Pastor Hank Hanley. She knew when the Parkinson's disease began to take over his existence and his ability to function. She also knew when the mental illness he harbored began to spiral out of control. She knew when he began to drink heavily to cope with the physical and emotional challenges. She knew when his drinking got the best of him. She knew about his mistresses and his love child. She knew when he went into the hospital first for a week and then for a month. She would fake continuing education and take care of all the paperwork. Rochelle also knew when Hanley needed to go into the hospital, when he needed his meds, when he needed to let go of the alcohol, and when he refused all means of help.

Rochelle knew when the beloved Pastor of Holy Hill began to shake and couldn't stop his hands from trembling. She had held his hand when he signed his name to official documents that the church officials really should have signed. She had even taught some of his seminary classes for him. She had sat silently as his family, the church officers, and the congregation refused to acknowledge that he should have retired fifteen years ago. When he refused to retire at all, he should have been forced out of office by whatever means was necessary. The people just couldn't make themselves force a beloved founding pastor out of office. He had been so powerful, so strong, and so charismatic. So everyone just sat back in denial.

Hank Hanley had baptized children, watched them grow up, married those children, performed funerals, and buried their parents and grandparents. He had seen so many of them go off to college, served as a reference for many, gone to court proceedings with the wayward ones, and written/sent money to any who was incarcerated. Then there were all the secrets that no one knew except Hanley and Rochelle. There were secrets Rochelle Mirabeau would take to her grave. For the heartbreaking reality of Holy Hill Church, just ask Rochelle Mirabeau. The only problem with asking was that you wouldn't get an answer. Rochelle knew what trust and confidentiality meant. She wouldn't talk. Rochelle knew where all the Holy Hill bodies were buried and she wasn't giving up the answers. Rochelle knew how the First Family of Holy Hill hid their secrets and judged the world in an attempt to keep their faults within the family. Rochelle KNEW.

Rochelle Mirabeau had come to Holy Hill as a young single mother of four children, needing a job. She had been laid off from her job with a local plant, and she wanted a position in which she could take care of her children and the organization. The church was a perfect fit. She had been able to begin work at 9:30 a.m. instead of 7:00 a.m., which meant she could see her children off to school and still have time to arrive at work on time. She had been able to talk with Rev. Hanley and be present for her children's soccer games, violin concerts, and plays at school. She had medical and dental benefits as well as a month off each year for vacation. She had a supervisor who had five of his own children who said, "Just let me know when you need to be off for the kids. I understand with five of my own." Wow, what a job!

Rochelle also knew this lovely woman, Pastor Rameeka. She knew that Rev. Rameeka might not have had a chance to survive beyond five years. Heck, she barely made it three. Rochelle had intervened in ways Rameeka would never know. She was glad to do it, and Rameeka would have been glad for her to do it. But Rochelle was a professional, and she knew exactly what to share and what not to share. She knew that this woman, the first and possibly the last female pastor of Holy Hill Church, needed help that only she could give. She was glad to give it.

Holy Hill Church was ruled and reigned by strong men who believed the place of women was in the home—barefoot, pregnant, cooking meals, spread eagled in the missionary position in the bedroom. She had told off many a Holy Hill Man who had decided she would be the mistress he wanted. She never sugar-coated words, and on numerous occasions Rochelle had watched Holy Hill Men walk away speechless, having been told off in no uncertain terms by a small no nonsense woman; they left wondering how to deal with her. They couldn't. She knew these men and what some of them expected when they saw a lovely woman who was single with children and no husband nearby.

Some Holy Hill Men assumed that since she was a widow and not wealthy that she would be starved for affection. What they didn't know was that Rochelle Mirabeau knew every trick any man would throw her way and how to send him on his way. Once the man made a move Rochelle would tell them exactly where to go and how soon they could get there. Most of them were married or engaged and looking for some side action. With Rochelle they were looking in the wrong place. She didn't care if she stomped on their egos or not because Rochelle was at Holy Hill for a specific purpose and it wasn't to sleep with the men. It was to serve God in Christ Jesus by being a great administrator for Christ's Church. If she needed to sleep with a man she knew where to go and to whom.

Rochelle was the de facto Associate Pastor or even Co-Pastor for Holy Hill Church. She had watched Hank Hanley deteriorate physically and mentally. She had kept extra vials of medication in her desk, the private phone number for Hank's psychiatrist, and she knew the back door to the private mental hospital up near Ventura. When Pastor Hank needed to be committed, she would quietly say, "Hank, it's time for a RIDE." Hank never refused. He understood. When his hands and arms shook from the Parkinson's, she would quietly take his papers, close the door to his office, and shield him from calls and appointments even if she had to reschedule them. She began to call herself "Rochelle the Protector".

Rochelle prepared all the bulletins for Sunday worship when she knew Pastor Hank Hanley could not provide the information. She would use the resources Hanley bought to assist him in preparing for worship. Rochelle read them from cover to cover so that she would do everything correctly. She would place lectionary information into the bulletin and study scriptures for sermon titles. She would tell Hanley what to preach and how to prepare his sermons. He would listen to Rochelle, but later he couldn't remember what she had said to him. He was too ashamed to ask her and most of the time he couldn't remember what to ask. Eventually his sermons were very different than they had been for the first forty years or so. They were disjointed, not organized, and the congregation had difficulty following him.

Many of the members, particularly the young adults, began to leave Holy Hill Church. Rochelle had watched it all, intervened when she could, and prayed that God would deliver the church so that it could be vital again. Of course the health of the congregation had to be restored. Could it? Maybe there were too many buried secrets. They would keep progress from taking hold. Buried secrets already had hindered the church's progress for many years. All Rochelle could do now was watch, speak when she could, and pray.

As was Rochelle's life practice, she made each moment a continual state of prayer. "Lord Almighty, bless this time in our lives. Be with Rev. Rameeka, protect her, heal her heart, and help her secure a new church. Gracious God, bless me. Forgive me for any actions I have taken at Holy Hill that may not have given you honor and glory. Lord, it was never my intent to keep secrets inappropriately or to make a situation worse by hiding anything. I was just trying to do the right thing. Lord, I know the claims the apostle Paul made about the thing we try to do right and end up doing wrong. Forgive me and set me on a straight path to follow you. Guide me in the way everlasting, and guide my pathway and my feet throughout the race of life. I pray all these things in the Name of Jesus Christ. Amen."

Rochelle came to grips with having kept painful secrets in the name of confidentiality. She thought she was doing the right thing at the time. She asked God's grace, mercy and forgiveness. Then she let go of her guilt and knew that a loving God cared for her in all circumstances, and had forgiven her completely.

Chapter 9

BURIED SECRETS

H oly Hill Church covered up many secrets for the sixty years it had celebrated this particular phase of its existence. The Church began in the shadow of a Euro-American church of the same name that began in 1900. That was old by Los Angeles standards. This first part of the history of Holy Hill Church was like many other congregations in the general Los Angeles Area that had their beginnings. A group of people began to meet often in people's homes, they would hold Bible Study, then they graduated to worship services; eventually they bought land and broke ground.

Some congregations began very differently than Holy Hill had begun. Some congregations rented space in other church buildings; other congregations rented space in hotels; still others rented or bought storefront buildings and built up the congregation from that point. Holy Hill Church met in the building that had once been a very different congregation by the same name. While the building needed a lot of repair, renovation and other work, the church building was paid in full so the congregation was responsible for the upkeep of the building itself.

Eventually it became a place that was brought up to code with the City of Los Angeles. Beginning a new phase of church history while carving out its own identity, positioned Holy Hill Church to do well. Holy Hill had been built as a community refuge and worship center for the community in which it was located. At that time, 1900, the particular area of Los Angeles was growing and progressing. Over the years as the community changed, Latino, Asian, and African-American families began to move into the area, began to purchase homes, and to raise families. As with many communities around the nation, many of the Euro-American families moved out. Historians, sociologists, and others labeled the movement "white flight".

The resistance to African-American families, other families of color, and their presence in the church itself led the families of Holy Hill Church to request closure from the region. Although the congregation was part of an independent denomination and was in charge of its own governance and policy, it was connected to a district and then a regional office. For reasons unknown or unspoken, it was the regional office rather than the district office that sanctioned the congregation's actions and approvals during the 1940s and 1950s. The church closed with three hundred fifty members who dispersed to become members of other congregations or not to become members of any.

Following the closure Holy Hill Church stood empty for three years. The district office maintained the building, allowed small groups to rent it from time to time, and cared for the surrounding property. In 1940 a pastor by the name of Delbert ("Dell") Wright came from Nebraska to be the pastor of Holy Hill. Dell was energetic and charismatic. He worked hard for ten years, and then left the ministry abruptly to sell insurance. He was very successful and opened an office in the general Compton Area. Once again Holy Hill Church was vacant and the care reverted to the district and regional offices.

Time continued to pass and the community forgot Delbert "Dell" Wright and that he had worked so hard to build Holy Hill Church. He became so successful as an insurance agent, broker, and businessman that people loved him in that role. Enter Hank Hanley. Hank Hanley moved to Los Angeles from Texas. The parsonage had deteriorated quite a bit after Dell Wright left. It was an old house and had serious repair needs. So Hank had to live in another location until the parsonage could be repaired. That took some time. After a few years he sent for his wife and two children. Hank was a young pastor, recently graduated from seminary with a dream for the church to flourish. Eventually he moved his family into the parsonage and began to work his dream. The Lord was with Hank in so many ways.

Hank was an outstanding preacher, pastor and prophet. He loved his work, loved the community, and loved the people. Hank was creative, courteous, and charismatic. The community responded to him in excellent ways. Hank convinced the community that Holy Hill was "their" church. In his interpretation for the people, God had created Holy Hill Church for the community, for the people, and for them to enjoy. He created excellent relationships with the business community, with the families, and with the community leaders. The church began to grow again in spite of the second closure following Dell Wright's departure. It continued to flourish so well and to become so strong and well known that Hank Hanley became a household name. Holy Hill Church was Hank Hanley's domain, kingdom, and world. The Church itself, Holy Hill Church, was Hank's mistress from the very beginning.

Hank ate, drank, slept, and breathed Holy Hill. His work became known throughout the entire area as he connected the church, community, and the business world in a way that built up the concept of partnership. Hank was a prominent figure in Civil and Human Rights, in the fight for equal rights in employment, housing, and Affirmative Action. He was a civic leader, a fighter for fairness, and one who loved African-American people. Hank united African-American, American Indian, Asian, Korean, Euro-American, Latino/Hispanic, and other people of color. He never excluded anyone; he loved all people no matter what their background. A multicultural presence would always be a reality where he lived and ministered; after all he was in Los Angeles. What a city of diversity. That was the heart and soul of progress. Hank worked hard to build the church into an institution that not only bore his name in heart and soul but that stood for ethics and integrity.

In the meantime Hank's family suffered. He was never home because he fought for others. He was never home because he was always with others. He was never home because he placed others first. The family became accustomed to his absence from the dinner table, the park, the school activities, and the family gatherings. Hank would sometimes cut family vacations short when someone died or was in the hospital. His sons would talk about what would happen when he would hang up the telephone from a call informing him that someone had passed away. The family would pack up their suitcases; get into their car, and drive back home. Hank placed the work of Holy Hill and the community before everything, even his health. What he didn't know was that his wife Amelia resented him with a vengeance that was so strong she began to have secret affairs with other men.

Sometimes these affairs weren't so secret, but Hank was oblivious because he had his own trysts. He was also was busy making life better for others. He was building up the kingdom of God. Sometimes the kingdom of God was confused with the kingdom of Hank. When human beings allow others to make them like gods, then one's own plans become what are interpreted as God's plans. Hank Hanley worked hard to be God's servant leader but he became such an icon that he became god to the people. Holy Hill Church was the Church of Hank Hanley, not the Church of Jesus Christ. There was a distinct difference.

While Hank became a god to the community and the church, Amelia was so angry that she became a mistress of several men over the years just to pay Hank back for ignoring her. Five grown children and sixty years later, she was still angry. Now she was an old woman whose life had become wrapped up in her husband's dreams. Her own dreams had faded into raising children, smiling at the countless faces in the church, and adorning Hank's arm at the numerous events to which they were required to attend.

Amelia had never worked, never fulfilled her own dreams of becoming a doctor, and now she was an 80 year-old widow whose husband never fully retired, had been mentally ill, drank too much, and had had Parkinson's to boot. When had anyone paid attention to her, listened to her, believed in her, or encouraged her to pursue her own goals. Amelia remembered Reuben, Sam, Alonzo, and Guillermo. They were among her past lovers who had listened to Amelia at least marginally. They were among the buried secrets that she assumed Hank didn't know. If he did know, he might not say anything. So Amelia assumed Hank didn't know about her buried secrets, or did he? If he knew, did he even care?

Amelia knew that she had to come to grips with her sinful actions and reactions. She knew that she had to seek God's intervention into her heart and soul. She began to ask God to ease her bitterness and to help her to release the anger with her husband. She finally realized that her anger toward Rev. Rameeka was a projection of her anger toward herself. After watching the committed members who were upset with her leave the congregation, she began to realize that repentance was necessary. She could pray in her heart and ask God to forgive, but she didn't have the courage to ask Rev. Rameeka to forgive her for all the lies, rudeness, and cruelty with which she had treated the new pastor.

Amelia felt that she would be too ashamed to approach Rameeka. She would have to deal with that guilt and shame. Maybe one day she would have the courage to approach Rev. Rameeka. Maybe one day Amelia would explain that she didn't know how to deal the radical changes in her life. Amelia grew up in an era and in a church that did not ordain women. Women were relegated to certain roles that in most cases were quite stereotypical. Women prepared the meals for Sunday dinners; women taught Sunday School for children and youth; women supported their husbands; and women were silent in church. The anger and frustration Amelia directed toward Rameeka mirrored her own upset with society, with the mindset of the church, and with her husband. Maybe one day Amelia could apologize to Rameeka. May one day she could explain to Rameeka that she had a lot of pent up aggression and shame about her life and her situation. However, today she just approached God and asked God to wipe the slate of sinfulness clean so that she could face the days ahead in heartfelt peace. Peace would be a long, hard road for Amelia. She just had to work on it day by day.

Chapter 10
MENTALITY OF MISTRUST

R ameeka rose to meet the day with a prayer and a song. God had seen her through the night, and God had blessed her to see another day. She had to be thankful. Thanksgiving was going to be her motto for the day. God was good all the time, God was always watching over creation, and God had provided Rameeka with a family who loved her, a group of friends who cared about her, and a vision that would take her far in life. She worked hard to be positive, to be forward thinking, and to be in a good spiritual place. It took hard work, but she kept working at it. She continued to beseech God to guide and keep her through the hard times.

Truly Rameeka was in a hard place with a lot of pain through which she had to work. She had prayed that the church's conflict would work itself out, but the truth was that the conflict had become a nightmare of accusations, gossip, rumors, and innuendos. A dissident faction began with Amelia Hanley and a small group of elderly, bitter, angry women who kept circulating their falsehoods and fabrications so that Rameeka would be discredited and her ministry would be in question.

The dissident faction wanted Rameeka out of the position. Actually they wanted more. They wanted to ruin her. How dare she come to Holy Hill and act so confident and smug? How dare she smile in the face of adversity and act as if nothing was going on. How dare she, an attractive woman who wore high heels, open-toed shoes, red nail polish and make-up, come to lead Holy Hill Church? As the dissidents stepped up the smear campaign, Rameeka smiled harder and seemed even more confident. They just made up more lies and acted out even worse. They kept the smear campaign alive. They would get her eventually. That was their commitment.

What the dissidents didn't understand was that in five years Rameeka had garnered love and support from so many members that the dissidents had been forgotten. That group wanted to be in charge of the church. It was their church. Some of them had been members for all of the sixty years Hank had been the pastor. He had brought many of them to faith. No one could lead like Hank. No one could minister like Hank. No one could be Hank. What a political mess.

When the group sent petitions and letters containing lies and rumors to the district and regional offices without contacting Rameeka, the church board, or to the executive committee chairperson Lana Burton, everything spiraled out of control. The dissidents felt that they would just go over Rev. Rameeka's head and show her who was really in charge. None of the dissidents had been in leadership nor had they served as officers during Rameeka's entire time at Holy Hill Church. No one had nominated them, and no one had promoted them. Several of them barely attended worship on a regular basis.

Most of that group had a reputation for being difficult even when Hank was the pastor. Some of them wrote individual letters to the district office and regional offices; some of them met with the district and regional office staff in person. Their purpose for meeting with the district and regional staff was to encourage Hank's dismissal. Their reason for wishing for him to be dismissed was that he was so ill he was unable to continue leading the congregation. Of course those who complained never complained to Hank personally. They complained about Hank, telling the district and regional officers that Hank needed to leave Holy Hill. Many of them did not understand that as an independent denomination, the offices did not remove pastors. Rameeka felt that the detractors had life issues and needs that were not addressed or reconciled. Instead of dealing with their issues they just kept acting out.

When people do not deal with their own life issues in therapeutic and healthy ways they may transfer their unhappiness onto others. Often the targets of the frustration have nothing to do with what is going on in the hearts of those who act out.

The disgruntled group acted out toward Rameeka, they held clandestine meetings, and printed brochures full of lies, then sent them to the district and regional offices.

When the offices received the slanderous petitions and letters it was then the offices responded to the dissidents. Later Rameeka remembered that neither office responded to the complaints about Hank. In Rameeka's estimation, the offices responded to the dissident group as if it were an official organization of Holy Hill Church, not realizing that the dissidents held no church offices, and had never been nominated to office during Rameeka's pastorate except for Timothy Haskins, who was not elected. Timothy was involved with the dissidents behind the scenes. He didn't sign the petitions, even though his wife Almeta did.

Timothy was a coward, had always been known as one who would never be direct in his concerns but who would plot in the background to bring about negativity. Timothy had come a long way in his life. He was born one of 11 children in abject poverty. He was raised in a very small rural village in South Carolina. He migrated to Los Angeles after his second marriage fell apart. He met Almeta while he worked for a railroad company. He was able to charm her and to convince her that he was much more than he was. She was from a wealthy family from Los Angeles, and had been a debutante and a socialite. However, Almeta had two strikes that hurt her in many ways. She was not bright or thoughtful, which were two states of being that hurt her socially and educationally.

Almeta and Timothy married at the age of about forty-five, and decided to make the best of their situation. Timothy was running for a political office in Los Angeles.

The election would take place before the next city council meeting, and Timothy didn't want his name officially involved in the deep conflict at Holy Hill. He was involved, however, and eventually the truth would emerge. It did. When the truth did emerge, it cost him his political reputation. He would never be elected to a city office. He would blame that reality on Rameeka also.

In addition, the regional director of the area in which Holy Hill Church was located had taken charge of this situation himself. He chose to be in communication with the proper committees and offices on an as needed basis. The regional director took most of the work upon himself, convincing himself that he knew just the path to take for Holy Hill Church. Green to the African-American culture, he thought he knew just what to do for this congregation. In his mind it was just like any other. Many Euro-Americans who worked hard to believe that racism was limited to overt actions were blind to the unconscious, unintentional decisions that plagued the world. They were oblivious to their privilege as Euro Americans. This director was no different. He could handle this church just like any other. All he had to do was to contact the higher authorities and move forward.

His decision-making was highly unusual and hard to figure. Rameeka wondered if he had dealt with other churches in any deep or meaningful way. District and regional directors always consulted the appropriate board, which was responsible for congregations in their areas.

Lana Burton was the executive chairperson, so she needed to consult the appropriate parties. She was responsible for those who were committee members assigned to the area in which Holy Hill was located. Then they would meet with the two assistant directors and the ministry enrichment team. That team would meet with the pastor and the church board.

Lana advised the team. In the case involving Holy Hill, the regional director had taken control of this situation, which left Lana on the sidelines of leadership. However, this time the regional director made decisions without consulting Lana or other appropriate parties. Rameeka felt that he made certain decisions that cost her and Holy Hill Church, but she had to deal with the fall out in the best way she could.

Holy Hill Church was part of a region of churches throughout Los Angeles and surrounding areas that had been grouped geographically. The geographical grouping was designed to promote fellowship, address business and other concerns, and to do so as an area with certain demographics in common. This region consisted of one 110 congregations that were overseen by a board of pastors headed by a district and a regional director. Rameeka's regional director was Royce Michelson. There were two assistant directors, namely Michael Ames and Carina Smythe; all were Euro-Americans who had no real understanding about the wealth of diversity of people who lived and worked in Compton, Gardena, and other nearby parts of Los Angeles. Lana Burton was a key figure as executive chairperson who advised the ministry enrichment team. Not one Latino was on staff, not one Asian, and not one African-American. There was one part-time American Indian who was the Financial Controller. He was only in the office on Tuesdays and Fridays.

Royce had been regional director for Southern Florida for three years. He was a retired lieutenant colonel who was accustomed to making decisions and to operating as he saw fit. He was somewhat new to Los Angeles, but had been criticized by many for working as a "lone ranger" and for making unilateral decisions. Rameeka tried hard to work with him, but his decisions had cost her and Holy Hill. All she could do at this point was to pray, prepare spiritually and emotionally to move on to another call, and to continue asking God's guidance. She wanted to trust the staff, but Michael Ames was the only person who seemed to understand and to care in a real way about what had happened to the church and what happened to Rameeka. Rameeka felt she had existed in a difficult system with a mentality of mistrust from the very beginning.

That lack of trust that Rameeka had felt since she began her ministry at Holy Hill Church had begun before she could begin her ministry there. During the final negotiations of her salary, start date, and other issues Rameeka learned that one of the finance committee members of Holy Hill Church, Monique Morris, eighty years of age and long retired from government work, had questioned the approval after Rameeka prepared to obtain a corporate credit card for business purposes. Monique asked, "Well, is she going to use it to buy clothes and perfume? Why does she need a corporate credit card?"

Rameeka told the chair of her search committee one thing. "Tell them to keep the damn card. I don't need to begin a ministry with such a spirit of mistrust." She never followed through with the request for the card. It had been approved already in spite of Monique; all Rameeka had to do was to decide which bank she wanted to use and obtain the card. She chose not to follow up with a corporate credit card because she didn't like the mentality of mistrust that she perceived existed before she could arrive. Rameeka had never used business funds for her personal needs. It could lead to trouble and it just wasn't the right thing to do. Later Rameeka learned that Hank Hanley had been provided with his own checking account from the church for discretionary purposes so that he wouldn't have to use his own money. Rameeka would never have accepted such an account even if the church had offered it. It just didn't feel right.

However, as pastor for sixty years Pastor Hank Hanley had long since had the trust of the Holy Hill congregation. Therefore, he did as he pleased when he pleased just the way he pleased. When one becomes an icon that person can call the shots. Hank was a shot caller and people responded in kind. Hank used the checking account however he wished with no questions asked and none answered. No one kept accurate church records, so there was no tracking of his spending. The church trusted him so there was no mention of the checkbook. Upon his retirement one church officer cleaned out Hank's desk and no one ever saw the checkbook again. At some point when members began questioning the lack of financial reports, Hank was reported to have said to several church officials that he "hoped there would not be an audit because a lot of people would be going to jail." Rameeka didn't know what that meant but later she would come to understand.

Rameeka would come to understand when she remembered that upon her entrée to Holy Hill Church she requested an audit for each year that an audit had not taken place. That was a total of fifteen years. The finance committee, led by Monique, began to hesitate about the audit. Monique stated that there were too many years in which there were no accurate records as well as years when there were no records, which anyone could review. Rameeka was flabbergasted at that first meeting of the finance committee five years ago. She remembered wise words from one of her mentors, a polite retired pastor. Larena had said, "Do not accept a call without reviewing audit reports for at least five years. Make certain they follow through and send you the information. If you don't see the audit reports and if you don't insist on it, there will be trouble." Rameeka didn't do that. She believed Timothy and the people who pushed her to accept the position at Holy Hill. They promised that when she came they would have an audit completed. That promise was one that was never fulfilled.

Rameeka blamed herself for being naïve and believing Timothy. He was not the chair of the search committee. He was a behind the scenes manipulator who believed that he would be Rameeka's favorite confidant. Since Timothy became one of the silent dissidents anyway, obviously there was never any intention of producing an audit. Rameeka prayed a silent prayer as she remembered the situation, "Lord, forgive me for my naïveté. Grant in me the wisdom to do things differently next time. Amen."

In the meantime, Rameeka spent her own money for business costs, and then try to remember to submit receipts to be reimbursed. Sometimes she would forget to submit the forms; sometimes she would submit the forms weeks late. She always seemed to be putting out money for the church and being reimbursed. Sometimes that wasn't so bad, but when she had to tie up her own cards to pay for dinners, hotel costs for visiting pastors and church leaders, and then take care of her own life it could be a hardship.

Then there were the community folk who came to the church for financial assistance. Providing financial assistance for the community was a mission outreach program of Holy Hill. Hank Hanley used to give money to community people who would come to his office regularly. Rameeka continued the ministry. One problem Rameeka discovered with the ministry was that there was no policy in place. In her mind the program was a "free for all". Rameeka had to carry large sums of money so that she could help them with utilities, rent, and other necessities. Most of the people who came to the church for help did not have bank accounts that would allow for a check to be written. They were cash and carry people, so a check would not be easy for them to handle. Thus Rameeka carried a lot of cash so that she could make life easier for them. That became a hardship.

So when the detractors wrote three petitions about Rameeka to the Regional Director's Office, financial impropriety was implied. That really devastated Rameeka. They didn't know how much of her own money Rameeka had spent helping people who came to the church, providing assistance for situations that were sometimes dubious, and giving away the church finances because the church had "always done that when Rev. Hank was there". Rameeka had given away at least as much as she had been reimbursed, if not more. Of course the accusation of embezzlement and theft upset her in a deep and hurtful way knowing what she did about the funds that the church provided. Rameeka became quite weary of carrying large sums of money, providing funds for unbelievable stories, and remembering to submit vouchers for reimbursement. It just wasn't worth the headache.

After the third year Rameeka discovered that the utility companies had special programs for people who needed additional assistance. For those who had a low income, were unemployed, or received public assistance there were special programs. Upon this discovery Rameeka told the Finance Committee that she didn't want to provide financial support for the community anymore. She told them why.

Rameeka didn't believe the preposterous stories that the people told to receive funds. She never had time to document the transactions properly, and this part of ministry was more appropriate for a small team of people who were equipped to complete the paperwork, interview those who requested the funds, and then to disburse them. What a responsibility for a pastor who had to visit the sick members, conduct funerals and provide overall care for the congregation, and conduct the four weekly Bible study classes that Rameeka facilitated. Somewhere in there Rameeka had to plan for Sunday worship.

Providing significant financial assistance for the community was too much for Rameeka. Maybe Hank had been able to do that; Rameeka had so many responsibilities. Hank had those same responsibilities, but Rameeka didn't like the dynamics. She didn't like not trusting the people when their stories didn't sound believable. She didn't like seeing the same people every month seeking additional funds. She didn't like the odd living situations that they shared with Rameeka when they requested funds for rent. The sad thing was that there were people who lived that way, and a lot of what the people shared could have been true. It was a shame that a nation that was called "The Land of the Free and the Home of the Brave" would allow and acknowledge that some people really did have to live that way. That's why Rameeka quietly carried cash and gave them the funds.

Rameeka thought about people like Teddy, for instance. He was born and raised in Compton and grew up in the general community of Holy Hill Church. Teddy attended all of the summer program experiences that Holy Hill Church sponsored from childhood through his teen years. He was about forty-nine when Rameeka met him. He used to come to the church several times a day just to use the restroom. The first time she saw him she asked if she could help him. He looked like a homeless man with his army gorilla outfit and backpack on his back. He said, "I'm just using the restroom." He went in and came out. Rameeka was a bit confused.

Teddy had grown up in the community, loved Holy Hill Church, never became a member, but claimed the church as his own. He came to Rameeka's office one afternoon about a week after Rameeka began, following the restroom incident. He introduced himself and said that he used to visit with Rev. Hank, who would help him out financially. Rameeka heard his story, how he never had a job but always looked out for Holy Hill Church. Rameeka knew that meant she would give Teddy money whenever he came to ask. However, Rameeka would ask Teddy to help out around the church and then she would give him $20, $30, or sometimes $50. Interestingly enough, Rameeka and her daughter were at the church one Saturday evening.

Rameeka was printing out her sermon to put finishing touches on it for the next morning. Her daughter was on Rochelle's computer checking emails. Someone banged on the door and when Rameeka went to the door she saw that it was Teddy.

"Pastor Rameeka I saw your car. Are you ok?"

"Yes, Teddy," Rameeka said as she opened the door to let Teddy in. "What do you need?"

"Nothing, I just saw your car and I know that you ain't never here this late. It is 6:00 p.m. It will be dark in another hour."

"Thanks Teddy. I'm ok. My daughter and I are just doing a little work before we go home."

"Well, lemme wait for you. I don't want anything to happen to you. This ain't the suburbs, Rev."

Rameeka said, "Oh that's ok Teddy. We are fine. We will leave in about twenty minutes."

"Rev., I ain't leavin'. I just want y'all to be ok. Please let me sit here in the hall and wait for you. I will just walk y'all to your car."

"Ok. Thanks Teddy. We won't be too long."

Rameeka went back into the office, and true to her word, she was ready to leave in twenty minutes. Teddy walked them to the car after Rameeka put the alarm on and turned off the lights. Teddy assured that Rameeka's car doors were closed and locked, he secured the church gate, and said, "Now y'all be safe going home Rev. Y'all don't know this neighborhood. I know y'all done lived in the suburbs. I can tell. This neighborhood ain't safe after about now. Now lock you doors Rev., and don't be stoppin' tryin' to help nobody. Be careful. See you next week."

Rameeka shook $20 into Teddy's hand and closed her car window. She and her daughter drove home realizing that this ministry was different than the others. They were indeed in the hood. This was Compton at the crossroads of Gardena and Los Angeles City. Taking care was the key word.

Well, that following Monday Rameeka saw two additional repair people that were unscheduled who came to the church because "Bill" called them. Did the church allow people to just walk in and out all day without knowing who had access? Rameeka supposed so. She assumed this fact because for her first three months at Holy Hill she walked into people no one knew who were all over the church claiming to be repairing things. Rochelle didn't know who was scheduled because the property committee made all the arrangements and never contacted the office to explain who was coming to provide services.

Well, that was one of the first changes Rameeka made. She met with the executive committee of the board and explained that it was unsafe for a church like Holy Hill to have arrangements made without notifying the office to make certain it was ok to send repair people. The executive committee took an action that was approved by the church board for anyone who came to the Church to report directly to the Holy Hill church office and for all repair people to contact the church office at least 24 hours in advance.

Holy Hill Church had a well-respected daycare program for infants to four years old as a community service program. Rameeka was deeply concerned about the children and who had access to the building. She worked with the executive committee so that the board took an action to require all people who came to the church to report to the office. The board also voted to lock all doors except for the front door and the back door where the children met daily. That action was major. It was an important change from what had been taking place. No wonder the detractors were angry. No more free for all access to the church; no more taking whatever they needed without anyone's knowledge.

What other changes were needed? Rameeka discovered what they were soon enough. She worked to make those changes with the appropriate committees over the few years of her service much to the chagrin of the old guard.

Chapter 11

REIGN, RULE, AND RUIN

H oly Hill Church was a church of proud, accomplished men. Some held Ph.D.'s, some held ED.D.'s, and others held advanced degrees of some kind, worked hard, and eventually moved to the surrounding suburban areas to purchase lovely homes. Others had worked hard to accomplish what they had even if they didn't have an opportunity to obtain advanced degrees. Many of the men and their families had survived and moved away from Watts, Compton, parts of Crenshaw, and other areas of Los Angeles that held hard memories for them from years past. However, one can physically escape one's surroundings but one can never escape the experiences of one's life.

Life experiences are marked on the soul. They become experiences from which we can learn, take to heart and use for future gain, or they can render us hurt, angry, and bitter when we are not able to overcome trauma or difficulty. Likewise joyful experiences are marked on the soul; they provide a place of comfort and strength. When a person moves to a new community, that person moves with experiences that are part of his or her soul. We take the memories with us, whether they are joyful or sorrowful. The life experiences that people carry are part of them. We can seek healing when those life experiences have been painful or we can use those experiences to develop a positive future. We can also use them for destruction. Both were the life experiences of Holy Hill member Lavon Jackson.

Lavon was born and lived in a small town in Arkansas. He lived in abject poverty, experienced the racism that was deep in the soul of the community and the world into which he was raised. He left for college at the age of seventeen, attended a small college for African-American students and graduated with a degree in Education. He promptly moved to Los Angeles, where his aunt and uncle were living and working. Soon Lavon was hired by a high school where he taught physical education, continued to attend classes for his Master's Degree at night, and eventually married his first wife, Paula. Paula and Lavon welcomed their daughter Helene into the world, and lavished her with every privilege that they never had in their childhood years.

Eventually Lavon discovered that he was attractive to the ladies and began to keep mistresses, which was quite expensive on a teacher's salary. When he completed his doctorate in the field of Education, Lavon was promoted to Assistant Principal then to Principal. He was quite good at what he did professionally and personally. The women sought him out and he always responded. Lavon's first marriage broke up and within six months after the divorce he married his second wife Marguerite.

Marguerite was completely opposite of Paula. Paula was quiet, enjoyed staying at home and didn't like to travel. She had been born and raised in Los Angles, and she didn't have a desire or a perspective for the rest of the country or the world. Marguerite was a socialite, loved parties, and enjoyed buying fine clothes. She had come to Los Angeles with her parents at the age of six. They moved from Texas seeking a better life for their only child. Marguerite learned social graces from her mother, and embraced the social life with passion. She could plan and host a social event that people would talk about for weeks. Then she could plan another to outdo what she had already done. Lavon and Marguerite had no children, so when he met Alicia, his third wife, the divorce from Marguerite was relatively clean and free from complications.

It was while he was married to Alicia that his financial troubles reached their peak. He learned the hard way that financial impropriety would result in difficulty for the perpetrator. Eventually Lavon was charged officially with financial impropriety by the Los Angeles City Board of Education. Some of the life lessons that are so crucial were beginning to penetrate Lavon's mind and heart. One of those life lessons was that being dishonest brings consequences that may result in public humiliation. Another life lesson Lavon learned was that when one plans to have a rendezvous with a fellow teacher, the plans should be made away from school property. Lavon was forced to take an early retirement and to leave the Education field altogether to avoid prosecution. He was dependent upon Alicia, who filed for divorce while she was pregnant with their third child, Lavon, Jr., his only son.

Alyssa was Lavon's first child with Alicia. He and Alicia had obviously enjoyed more joyful times in their relationship. Lavon had three marriages, three children, and was trying to live down his reputation as a philanderer. It didn't work because Lavon continued to date women outside of his marriage. Eventually Alicia divorced Lavon, took the children and moved to Alexandria, Virginia with her cousins. Lavon was alone, experiencing financial difficulty, and getting older.

Lavon Maurice Jackson was eighty when Rameeka met him at Holy Hill Church. She remembered him because he was always making off color remarks to the women. The church was quite accepting of Lavon's behavior, explaining it away as, "Oh everyone knows Lavon. He's just playing around." Eventually one woman did not take Lavon's advances as a mere joke. Rameeka remembered learning about Lavon and his life situations that led up to his present time at Holy Hill Church.

At some point during his tenure as a principal, Lavon was caught with a teacher in a compromising position. At the same time the school district began to press charges regarding the financial issues. That was when his wife spent her life savings to retain a lawyer who was able to

settle everything without going to court and without prosecution. The Los Angeles City School District dropped
the charges against Lavon; however, Lavon was forced
to retire. He spent his retirement going from one mistress
to another. Some reports circulated that Lavon's women
would leave a piece of lingerie in his car following their
dates. It became their calling card.

Alicia became fed up with the 'calling cards' and filed
for divorce after 8 years. Lavon, Jr. was three years old.
With his money gone and his career shot, Lavon rented
a small apartment and went to work for a small trucking
company as a dispatcher. He never could leave the women
alone. Even at eighty years Lavon served as a greeter at
the church and fondled women as he provided them with a
bulletin on Sunday mornings. He wanted to provide them
with something else, but most of them laughed at him.
The rest of the women just quietly never returned to Holy
Hill Church. They told their friends to stay away from the
church with the crazy man who tried to 'cop a feel' as he
handed out bulletins on Sunday mornings.

Some of the Holy Hill Church members were displeased
with the way Rev. Rameeka dealt with Lavon Jackson. In
their minds he was a fine man who had been part of the
church since the early days. If everyone else ignored him
and his advances on the women, then why couldn't the
woman who reported him just deal with Lavon? After all,
she should have laughed like everyone else and just walked
away. The other women had laughed and gone about their

business. Some of them had admitted being offended but just kept quiet. In those cases Lavon would approach them over and over again knowing that someone would allow him to spend time with them.

What about the non-church members who had visited Holy Hill Church on a Sunday morning just seeking to worship, possibly decide upon a church home, or who may have been visiting their friends? Those women attended worship with no intention except to enjoy the service. They had been hit on by Lavon. Many of the members felt that people should have known that Lavon was just flirting innocently and he was just a people person. After all, that was how Lavon explained things. He just liked to have fun; he was an outgoing person. In the minds of those who supported Lavon and whatever he did was only done in jest. The members felt that the women who visited just may have decided to go somewhere else anyway. They had the privilege of deciding that Holy Hill Church may not have been their choice. Previously, no one had complained about Lavon in an official capacity. The women just complained among themselves and told no one about his inappropriate behavior. Why now? The secret of Lavon Jackson became so deeply buried in the soul of Holy Hill Church that no one ever discussed it. They just endured.

One question Rameeka continued to ask in her prayers and meditation was this question: Where was the remorse and where was the apology? Even if Lavon had not meant to offend but felt that he was just being a man, was there anything in his heart that could have led him to say, "If I have offended anyone I apologize." Even though for Rameeka that was a backhanded way of apologizing, at least he would have mentioned the word. Lavon never seemed to be apologetic or remorseful. Rameeka wondered if another pastoral conversation with him would help him to see that he needed to be more guarded and disciplined about what he said to women. She tried a few more pastoral care discussions with Lavon; they didn't work. He regularly denied any inappropriate actions and referred to himself as a "people person" who just liked to have a good time. All Rameeka could do was to pray for Lavon, continue meeting and talking with him.

One way in which Rameeka dealt with the Lavon Jackson was to encourage the ushers to develop a method of operation so that all ushers knew how to operate. They developed a training program with educational components built into the program. Rameeka taught the educational components; she taught theological concepts of what ushering and hospitality were supposed to accomplish. Those who did not participate could not serve until they completed the educational training. The position of usher was an important position; it had to be honored and treated that way. In order for respect for an usher to take place, the usher had to carry himself or herself with dignity and respect for others and for him/herself. The church board approved the ushers' educational program with vigor and unanimity.

If Lavon wasn't enough there was Aaron Morrow. Aaron was the fine church man who had volunteered for youth ministry, worked with the Men's Ministry, and who had gone out of his way in community outreach. Aaron Morrow was married to Maureen, a former model and photographer. They had been happily married for forty-two years, and were active in all church activities. They gave generously to the building campaign, had chaired the building of the youth activity complex, and taught Sunday School. Aaron had been a small business owner who became very successful. His dry cleaning company had become a franchise all over the Greater Los Angeles Area as far as Pomona and Victorville. When Aaron retired, his son and daughter took over the business and expanded the cleaners to Oxnard, Ventura, and San Diego.

The Morrow Family was well loved and respected. Maybe that was why the secret gossip about Aaron's love for young teen and pre-teen boys was not addressed. One morning a young handsome high school student, Ross Andrew Wayne, was asked to perform during the afternoon concert. Ross majored in music. He played the violin like an angel from heaven. He was very talented, very polite, but shy and distant. One day Rev. Rameeka discovered why.

Following Bible Study John Mayberry approached her and asked if they could have lunch. Rameeka never said no to her people if she was able to make a meeting in any way. Lunch was her favorite meal because she had missed it so often. Self-care was a challenge for Rameeka and she would work hard to do better. So when John asked Rameeka to have lunch she consented. Leaving the church building for lunch was a way Rameeka could tell herself that she was practicing "self-care". Rameeka and John left church and drove to a nearby Thai restaurant. Why did Rameeka have a feeling that this lunch was not a routine fellowship? She would soon find out.

John Mayberry had done his homework well. Rev. Rameeka loved Thai food, sushi, "sake", and soul food. She was a fiend for tamales so John had a plan to take his pastor to every one of the restaurants that she loved. He and his wife knew all of the good places. John loved to drive out past Santa Monica to a fine Thai restaurant that overlooked the ocean. It was right on the beach. Today he needed to provide a comforting atmosphere for what he had to tell her.

John loved his pastor, and he appreciated her leadership. He and his wife wished she had more time to spend at their home for dinner and visits. However, they were grateful for the time she did have to spend with them. John wished this lunch could have been a celebration lunch. However, it was not; John had a lot on his mind.

John and his wife Denise were retired social workers who had served the County of Los Angeles for twenty-eight years. They met at the main office where both of them worked. They were instantly attracted to each other. They dated for about ten months, became engaged, and were married five months later. John and Denise worked together until they retired. Known as the model for love and fidelity, John and Denise taught relationship seminars and workshops. They had studied relationship building and couples therapy for many years until they became licensed to counsel and provide workshops for couples who were planning to wed and those who had already wed.

John Mayberry was a native of Los Angeles. His family traced its history back to the founding of Los Angeles. As a family, the Mayberrys were proud of the active presence in the establishment of such a fine city. Denise was a native of Puerto Rico; her family moved to Florida then to Los Angeles when Denise was three years old. The Mayberry family visited Puerto Rico at least twice a year since their marriage. This way Denise could remain in regular contact with her family who remained in Puerto Rico. Her family visited Los Angeles regularly also in order to maintain family connection and communication. Family was essential for the Mayberrys.

John and Rev. Rameeka were seated. They had an excellent location by the window. John was glad to take Rameeka upscale to one of this particular Thai restaurant so that he could really explain what she needed to know. After they ordered, John made small talk. Rameeka was nothing if not perceptive, so when she noticed that John was talking about trivial things, she simply said, "John, what's wrong? If there is something important I need to know please tell me. Are you ill, or is Denise in need of anything? What can I do to help, whatever it is?"

"Rev., there is a situation that is painful for me to mention but I have to tell you. I don't know where else to go. Ross Wayne has become close to Denise and me over the last year. He came by the house this morning and asked to talk with me. He told me that Aaron Morrow began molesting him when he was twelve and it continued until last year when he turned seventeen. I know the system and how it works because I am a mandated reporter like you, but I really want you to know that I have contacted the police and made an official report with Aaron. You have to know as the pastor that it is not safe for Aaron to be around the youth.

His behavior has been rumored for several years, but no one would say or do anything. I have not been involved with the youth work until early this year and I have remained close to the youth and to Ross. Ross told me officially, and when I asked him if he knew that I had to make the report he said he wanted to make the report himself but he wanted me to go with him."

Rameeka sat back and took a deep breath. She felt as if a boulder had bounced from her chest to her head and back. Here was another mess for her to address. The sexual acting out and misconduct were prominent themes at Holy Hill Church. Several of the men at Holy Hill had been in complete control of their families and their lives until someone got caught doing wrong. Hank Hanley had never been caught or whispered about in any sexual scandal, but Rochelle knew every mistress he had taken since he served Holy Hill. Rameeka discovered several of them when they came to her to confess and to seek assistance. Rameeka prayed with them, provided as strong a program of pastoral care as she could possibly provide, and encouraged them to continue to seek out God's guidance and wisdom in their own lives. Most of the former mistresses belonged to other congregations. Two were un-churched, but were seeking a place of spiritual refuge. They were all seeking acceptance and love. Sometimes people seek love and acceptance in unhealthy and non-spiritual ways. However, since all humanity is sinful, we rely upon God's forgiving grace in Jesus Christ. No one was perfect and no one was in a position to pass judgment. Rameeka shared that reality with each woman in the most pastoral manner she could.

As Rameeka discovered, many of the men at Holy Hill Church had reigned, ruled, and ruined certain aspects of ministry as well as their own families. That was a story for another chapter. Right now she had to deal with Aaron Morrow and what was coming next.

Rameeka looked at John and asked him if he was all right. "Yes, Pastor, I'm fine physically, but spiritually and emotionally I am in deep pain. How does a man molest youth in the church and no one seems to know or care?"

Rameeka took a deep breath and prayed with John. They had a lot of work to do for the church and for the families. Ross grew up in the church, was part of the youth group, Sunday School, and in the Youth Choir. Aaron had significant contact with so many of the youth. Rameeka was going to spend sleepless nights and she would miss many meals. She had to care for a congregation that had a sexual predator who had preyed upon children. That would surely tear up a congregation.

John and Rameeka finished lunch and drove back to the church. John left his pastor at the front door of the church and promised to see her at the Board meeting. Rameeka was going to have to call an emergency meeting to deal with the issue. Rameeka walked into the office with Ross on her mind. Rochelle was hanging up from a call.

"Hi Rameeka. You just had a call from Chief Andrew Stone. He would like for you to call him right away."

"Ok. Thanks." This call could only mean that the Chief of Police wanted to talk about Ross Andrew Wayne and the situation with Aaron Morrow.

"Rochelle, please see if you can get him back on the phone for me."

"Sure."

Chapter 12

WHAT NOW?

C hief Andrew Stone had worked for the Los Angeles Police Department for his entire career. He was upstanding, direct and honest. He was a good police officer; he detested child molestation and had learned of a tragic instance involving a young man named Ross Andrew Wayne. In this instance he needed to speak with Rev. Rameeka Middlebrooks to understand what she knew. The young man, Ross Wayne, had reported that several instances had taken place on church property. The Chief really needed to talk with the Pastor.

Chief Stone had taken the report himself. It stated clearly that a longstanding professional had sexually abused a young male child from the age of twelve to seventeen. These reports were always disturbing and deserved imme-diate attention. There was something about this report that really captured his attention. When he spoke with Ross and the older gentleman who accompanied him Chief Stone believed Ross immediately. That didn't usually happen with the Chief; he was naturally suspicious of some and wary about the stories of others. He always listened for stories to have something that didn't sound true. However, Chief Stone had excellent instincts and found young Ross Wayne quite believable. As Chief Stone sat back in his office his assistant put a call through to him.

"Hello Chief Stone. This is Rev. Rameeka Middlebrooks returning your call."

"Yes ma'am. Good afternoon. Thank you for returning my call. I would like to meet with you regarding a young man by the name of Ross Wayne. I believe he is a member of your congregation. He came to see me today."

"Yes. I have been made aware. I would be happy to meet with you."

"I will come to your office. How is the rest of your afternoon?"

"I am in the office until 6 p.m. this evening. Anytime is convenient."

"Thank you Rev. I expect to see you in about an hour."

"Thank you Chief. See you when you arrive."

"Goodbye."

Rameeka hung up and prayed hard and long. She had not heard of the whispers about Aaron Morrow nor had she been in the gossip line of Holy Hill Church. As the Pastor she worked hard to stay out of the line of gossip, but child molestation, statutory rape, child sexual abuse, and any violation of youth and children pained Rameeka. She loved children and always enjoyed their company. To think of any of them being hurt disturbed her. If Aaron Morrow actually committed this atrocity it would rock the church beyond its ability to be objective and fair. This tragedy had the ability to destroy the tranquil façade the church had been displaying for many years. That façade could no longer cover over the volcano that was about to erupt among the congregation or in the community. There was no way the community could be kept from knowing about this tragedy. Aaron Morrow was known throughout the Southern California Area from Ventura/Oxnard to San Diego. Rameeka knew that the news media would get ahold of this story somehow and it would rock the entire Southern California Coast.

The story was beginning to remind Rameeka of another story she had heard from several sources. It related to George Harrison Taylor, a less than faithful member of Holy Hill Church. George was a retired Security Officer for one of the community colleges in the area, had a reputation that was less than positive, and thought very highly of himself. His wife, Seville, was fiercely protective of George, especially those times when he was accused of molesting or attempting to molest young girls. Seville never believed anyone who accused George of inappropriate behavior and she always berated any female, teenager, adult or otherwise who seemed to have any relationship with George.

George Taylor was reported to have approached and touched four teenage daughters of three single parent members of Holy Hill. The approaches reportedly took place about twenty years prior to Rameeka's entrée to Holy Hill Church. One girl, Saffina, was about fifteen at the time of the alleged approach. She was reported to have shared the incident with Amelia Hanley, who had befriended Saffina's mother. Amelia was reported to have told Saffina to say nothing to anyone and to make certain not to go near George again. After her graduation from high school Saffina went away to college, accepted a position as a teacher in Atlanta, GA, and never returned to Los Angeles.

Saffina's sister, Rose, told her mother about George's approaches upon her. Rose and Saffina's mother reportedly took a sawed off shotgun and waited outside of George's home until he came from work. As George got out of his car, Saffina and Rose's mother approached him with the shotgun clicked and ready for shooting. She threatened to shoot off George's "family jewels" if he ever approached her children or anyone else's children in the church. It was said that Rose and Saffina's mother hurled several other insults at George, then unclicked her shotgun, got into her car, and drove home. No reports about George approaching teen girls ever surfaced at Holy Hill again. Rameeka found herself wondering if he just chose young girls who were not part of the church. George was now seventy-seven years of age, but the way he seemed to look at the teen girls who were part of Holy Hill disturbed some of the people. Even though it disturbed them, no one ever spoke a word. No one wanted to bring anything negative to Holy Hill's reputation in the community of Los Angeles.

Holy Hill Church was elite and quite proud of its history in Civil Rights and its reputation as a middle-class, well-educated congregation, mostly because of the work of Hank Hanley. However, the buried secrets were slowly boiling over and it would be next to impossible to cover them up. Rameeka remembered the old adage, "What is done in darkness will come to light." The light was beginning to shine.

The situation involving Aaron Morrow could and would become quite public; it would probably never be covered up. The local newspaper, community newspapers, television news, and the most effective "word of mouth" network would be at work telling the story of Aaron Morrow and his sexual violation of young boys. Rameeka's concerns were real and quite valid. The fall out behind the publicity would be quite difficult to address.

Holy Hill Church would not take kindly to any negative publicity about the members, especially anything that involved being arrested, jail time, sexual misconduct, or anything that might keep people from becoming members. The members would do whatever they could to save what they saw as a good reputation of the church. Holy Hill Church would sacrifice Ross to save Aaron. Aaron was rich, older, and savvy. Ross was young, poor, shy, and he would be no match for a professional like Aaron. Yes, it would be hard for some to believe Ross even if the story was true. It would be easy for Holy Hill members to believe Aaron even if he lied. Holy Hill members covered up for each other for the most part and refused to believe bad things even if they were true. If the person was financially well to do and supported Holy Hill, then then no one would deal with the issue. They valued the financial gifts more than scandal. That was Holy Hill.

Rameeka sat down with the Chief in her office for tea and conversation. She shared what she knew, which was that John Mayberry had shared the accusation with her with Ross's permission. John Mayberry and Rev. Rameeka Middlebrooks were mandated reporters, which meant that if they knew or were informed of abuse they had to report it. John had also mentioned that Ross Wayne wanted to sit down with Rameeka for pastoral care and counseling. Rameeka was planning to meet with Ross that evening, which was why she would be at the office until 6 p.m. Chief Andrew Stone would be following up with Rameeka and with Ross.

As they ended the meeting Chief Stone expressed his sorrow at the situation and offered his help in any way possible for Rameeka and the congregation. Rameeka would be utilizing his assistance. She had already thought about small group forums with district representatives facilitating the groups. She thought about asking her friend and colleague Yvette to lead an all church retreat on rape/ sexual misconduct. She would take this information to the church board for its review and approval. Something had to be done to stop the child abuse. More than anything the church had to deal with the issue. That would be a challenge because Holy Hill buried its secrets deep and hard; the church would roll on as if there were no problems.

Of course when an organization pretends that issues don't exist, that organization cannot thrive and it cannot survive. A church that buries its secrets and allows privileged members to reign, rule, and ruin others is a church that ruins itself. So many young families left Holy Hill Church when the older scandals began to surface. Then other young adults left when Hank Hanley could not function and no one would face the reality of what needed to be done. Rameeka thought long and hard about how to handle the upcoming volcano that was about to erupt. She remembered the words of mentors long past, "Denial leads to difficulty."

"Chief, I am thinking hard about having some small group forums about child abuse, how to report it, and what symptoms the victims display. I will be talking with the church board. Will you come and speak first to the board, then to the entire congregation?"

"I'd be happy to do that as long we can have tea again and as long as you know you can call on me whenever and for whatever you need in this arena. Let me do as much as you need."

"Ok. We have a good agreement. Thanks."

"Goodbye Rev."

Rameeka noticed that Rochelle had left for the day, and she turned off the light in Rochelle's office. She walked back into her own office, sat down, said a prayer, and leaned back in her chair.

As she sat deep in thought, Rameeka received a telephone call from another member in crisis.

"Rev. Rameeka, this is Marlena Menendez. I have to see you. My husband beat me again and this time I am serious about the shelter. Please help me."

"Why don't you come to my office now? Can you do that? Where are you?"

"Not far away. I am on the corner of Rosecrans and Central. I took my car and I can be there shortly. I left while Eddie was sleeping. Pastor Rameeka this time I am not going back."

"Okay Marlena. I will make a call to the women's space while you come on over. Don't worry about anything you don't have with you. Either the women's space or I will take care of it all."

Marlena was on her way and Rameeka tore open a granola bar someone had given her. As the telephone rang, she picked it up wondering what was happening on the other end this time.

"Holy Hill Church, Pastor Rameeka speaking."

"Pastor, I really need to talk with you."

"Certainly. Tell me who you are and how I can help."

Rameeka sat down at her desk wondering to herself, "What now?"

Chapter 13

RELEASE-A BREATH OF FRESH AIR

R ameeka left Holy Hill on time for a change. No matter what time she left the Church the traffic was Los Angeles' style traffic. The 110 was particularly bad that day. She always knew when traffic was particularly heavy in Pasadena. She could tell every time she reached Arroyo Parkway as the 110 ended in Pasadena. It was more than bumper to bumper, but Rameeka maneuvered her way over so that it wasn't as heavy as it could have been. Her "cruise" up Lake Avenue was bumper to bumper also. That was the way it was in the Greater Los Angeles Area. Lots of traffic, lots of accidents, lots of people all the time. Rameeka drove to her garage, hit the remote, and entered. She walked up the stairs and opened the door to her town-home. In Rameeka walked, maneuvering Fritzie's happy barking while tearing down the stairs to see her. He danced on his hind legs wagging his tail. This was his message that he was glad to see her and also needed a walk.

"Hello, Sweetie, how are you? Did you miss Grandma?" Fritzie barked twice and stood up on his hind legs. That meant that he really needed to walk. Rameeka sat her purse down, changed her shoes and put on Fritzie's leash. As she locked the door Fritzie began running. Rameeka gently pulled the leash, but her little Maltese/Shitzu kept moving. She picked up her speed to keep up with him. Marina, one of the leasing agents from her complex was driving potential clients on the open cart as they went to see an apartment.

Marina called out to Rameeka. "Hi, Pastor. Is Fritzie taking you for a walk?" Everyone laughed and Fritzie kept moving.

Rameeka walked with her little pooch and prayed that God would continue to bless the church, her family, her ministry, the community, and the world. Walking had always been a means of spiritual retreat for Rameeka. When she did not take her cell phone with her she was unavailable to the world; she could pray, relax, think, plan, and enjoy times of solitude. These days her walks with Fritzie provided a way to deal with all that had occurred. In spite of all that happened, Rameeka was remarkably calm. Although she was no longer the pastor of Holy Hill Church, Rameeka held no ill will toward any of the dissidents. She felt that the church had been in grief that had never been resolved. These days, however, were set aside for Rameeka's own healing and peace of mind.

Rameeka's daily walks with her daughter's dog provided solace, silence, rest, and release. She could release some of the pressure of a church gone wrong and ask God to make it all right. She could take some time for herself without the telephone ringing or someone coming to ask for money or members coming to share their issues with her. This time, this walk around the complex and through the park provided a time of renewal and relaxation for Rameeka. This time was her time and she took advantage of it at every opportunity. Twice a day, morning and evening, were standard walk times for Fritzie. Three times, if she could work it in, was an added blessing. If she could manage four walks in a day for Fritzie, both of them were in heaven.

The walks Rameeka took with Fritzie allowed her to realize how much she needed to rest, to relax, to be renewed, and to be rejuvenated. Those things would not happen without concerted effort on her part. She always talked about self-care for clergy. She even taught self-care with enthusiasm when she led new clergy orientation sessions. Self-care was crucial if she was going to be successful in any ministry. Rameeka realized that she had not taken good care of herself. Rameeka had worked long hours at Holy Hill Church. She had come into the office on her days off. She had not slept well at night; she had worked in the wee hours of the morning sending emails and writing proposals and reports at 3:00 a.m. That had to stop if she was going to be healthy and able to keep working.

Finally Rameeka realized that she was a perpetual workaholic. Her workaholic ways had taken their toll upon her children, other family members, her friends, and her own soul. It was time to do something better for herself. Rameeka's good friend of twenty-four years had called her the night before and left a voicemail. "Hey 'Meeka, it's Amy. I know about a cruise for ten days in November. Let's go, and because it's a wedding that will take place on the cruise I think I can arrange for you to do a prayer as part of the ceremony. The couple is a lovely young couple just out of college, and will be settling in Los Angeles. I know they will enjoy getting to know you. I told them about your church and they are very interested. They would fit just right in with the people. I know I can schedule you to conduct some premarital counseling for the couple in addition to what I do so maybe you can write off the trip. I know you love Bible Study, so if you want, maybe you would be willing to conduct a small forum on marriage or something and that would be good for your CPA to review when it is time to do your taxes. Call me back and let me know."

Ahhh, that Amy. Always putting people together and looking at some way to get some good, legitimate write offs. That was good! Rameeka knew she would call her dear friend back. They would be on that cruise and she would really be able to relax. In the meantime Rameeka ran with Fritzie and gave thanks for this small amount of time and refuge. "Thank you, Lord, for this time of rest and release. Amen."

Chapter 14

REDEMPTION

On the following Sunday morning after Amy's telephone call, worship ended and the congregation left Solid Rock Church where Rameeka had been the guest preacher for the morning. Her friend and colleague, Myron Wellman, had taken some much needed time away. He had called Rameeka to preach for him which kept her involved with the life of a congregation. Myron was a fine pastor, the church was healthy, and they welcomed Rameeka with enthusiasm.

The welcoming congregation responded very well to Rameeka's style and manner in the pulpit. There was an added value to the morning when Rameeka looked up and saw more than one hundred members of Holy Hill Church visiting in the assembly. They filled up the church, smiled at their former pastor and affirmed her presence and her work for the morning. God had smiled upon the people that morning, and more than that God had smiled upon Rameeka.

Rameeka took that affirmation with her into the week. It had done her heart good to see so many supporters in the congregation. She knew she was loved by many Holy Hill members. The presence of so many people made her smile and thank God for such means of grace. That week Rameeka took extra time completing applications for a new call, making connections, cleaning out her boxes and old paraphernalia. She didn't need to carry the past into a future call. It was time to let go. Rameeka's daughter was always telling her that. She was right. It was time to let go of the past so she could embrace the future with a new perspective and a healthy heart. In Rameeka's mind, that was redemption.

Rameeka knew what scars on a person's soul could do. She had worked with dozens of clients when she was in mental health whose scars on their souls didn't heal. Healing was therapeutic; it was a way to release hurts, painful situations and painful memories. Healing old hurts could help a person deal well with new challenges. So many members of Holy Hill Church carried scars upon their souls—scars that didn't get the healing medicine that could have rendered their frames of mind stronger and better able to take a healthy view of life. Most of them never received the help they needed in order to heal. All of Rameeka's efforts for the healing of the scarred hearts and souls of Holy Hill Church seemed to be in vain.

Rameeka remembered that once she preached a sermon entitled, "Healing Old Hurts", which was a two-part series designed to awaken the minds of others to the importance of seeking out healthy ways of putting old hurts aside. There were members of Holy Hill Church who had been raised in foster homes where severe abuse had rendered them unable to deal with life effectively. Some other members grew up in homes with parents and other family members who ridiculed them mentally, emotionally, verbally and physically. Often they carried out that same abuse on their children and upon others' children.

The chairperson of the church executive board used to say, "Hurt people hurt." People who are hurting hurt others and they hurt themselves. Sometimes they are aware and cannot help themselves, sometimes they are not aware and don't understand what they may have done to someone else. People who are hurting from the scars of life that may have penetrated their hearts and souls often lash out and hurt others. People who are angry about life's disappointments and difficulties pass that anger on to others, like family, friends and colleagues. People who turn their anger inside until it becomes guilt will impart that state of being onto other people when they least expect it.

Rameeka's members were often unaware of how angry and bitter some of them were. They carried that bitterness into every facet of their lives. While counseling might have helped the people to put things into perspective and to move on with life, most of them had never followed through with counseling because they felt they could handle things on their own. Some communities carry stigmas about counseling and mental illness, which often keeps people from discussing it or treating it. Individual and group counseling will take people a long way in dealing with scars on their souls if such counseling is sought. That counseling and/ or therapy would allow the scars to heal in ways that are redemptive, redeeming, and rewarding.

Rameeka knew that the imprint from scars on the soul left their mark in a person's heart and mind. Such trauma leaves its effect. Effective treatment results in healing of the scars. As such, a person can deal with life more effectively. Remembering how effective the right counseling could be, Rameeka had arranged for mental health professionals, hospital chaplains, and other pastors to address Bible study classes and special forums at the church. In addition she referred some of her members for more in-depth therapy. The problem with some of the special events for counseling and mental health issues was that those who really needed the help never attended. That was something Rameeka knew could happen. All she could was to pray and ask God to heal the scars on their souls.

Scars and hurts that are addressed in productive ways are God's way of providing redemption; healing is a means of grace. The healing and comforting presence of the Holy Spirit can work in and through our hearts, minds, and souls to effect the change in our ability to face life, to face others, and most of all to face ourselves. Scars on the soul can heal if one is willing to take the first step and to do the hard work. Rameeka was doing the hard work for herself; she refused to carry any hurt, anger, sadness, or bitterness into the next phase of her life and work. All she could do was to pray for those who would not help themselves. By not helping themselves through groups, forums, or therapy they were hurting themselves. In so doing, they were still carrying the scars upon their souls.

Chapter 15

WITH SCARS ON MY SOUL

How deep must the heartbreak be to leave scars on one's soul? For pastors like Rameeka who give everything they have, sometimes neglecting their own lives to care for others, the heartbreak goes deep and broad. It infiltrates the heart and mind, creating a pain that takes prayer, counseling, and hard work to overcome. For Rameeka, one who was prone to giving everything she had in a relationship to make it work, the scars on her soul would take time to heal.

Rameeka reflected on the scars her heart and soul had experienced. She was on the other side of the deep pain now, but that took some short-term counseling, additional exercise in the workout room, long walks with her friends and her daughter's dog, and all the prayer she could lift up to God. She was one who would bombard heaven with nonstop prayers and meditation for as long as she could remember. This experience brought her closer to a Lord who guided her through one of the deepest valleys of her life. Rameeka reflected upon everything she could bring to memory about God's goodness during her Holy Hill experience. She remembered the last Sunday she spent at Holy Hill Church.

She remembered the small group of dissenters, most of whom never came near her to shake hands. She remembered Ron Whiteside whom many said assisted in heading up the plot to destroy Rameeka's career. He approached her, shook hands, and talked incessantly about how he wished her well. "Well, Rev., I'm sorry things didn't work out. I don't know if you will remain active in the wider church. Maybe I'll see you around at some of the meetings. Uh, uh, I don't know if I'll see you around but uh, uh, well...." It was very clear to Rameeka that Ron was attempting to assuage his guilt and his ugly behavior with all of the incessant talking. She just watched as he talked and talked. While his eyes focused upon anything except Rameeka, she realized that Ron couldn't look her in the face with any ease or directness.

Rameeka froze a smile on her face and merely said, "God bless you. I will pray for you." She would not engage in conversation with Ron. It was meaningless.

Rameeka remembered that Ron had called her when she was in her previous position, tried to talk her into accepting the position to Holy Hill Church, then later became angry when he wasn't voted onto the church board. Rameeka wondered why he was calling her in New Mexico, and she even asked him that on a couple of occasions. Rameeka felt that it was highly out of order, and could create expectations that were not advisable. Maybe he thought that Rameeka owed him something since he had put all that effort into supporting her behind the scenes. Rameeka never sought that support from Ron. Rameeka never sought to obtain positions by working behind the scenes. Such actions always created situations that could end in disaster.

Ron operated differently. He liked the "good old boy" operation; maybe he didn't know any other way. As Ron talked on and on Rameeka reflected for a moment about what she knew of him. She remembered him from previous work on the national level. Ron had a reputation as a cutthroat and one who always take care of himself at anyone else's expense. Rameeka was one who did not listen to or thrive on gossip or word of mouth stories about others, but in this case Rameeka surmised that the word about Ron was quite truthful. She could point to her own personal experience with him as one excellent example.

Rameeka never sought Ron's support while she was being considered for Holy Hill; in fact she never sought the position at Holy Hill Church at all. Others had encouraged her to consider that call. Holy Hill Church had sought for Rameeka, and not the other way around. Rameeka was quite suspicious of Holy Hill because of the length of time that Hank Hanley had been the pastor. When she discovered that the church had not had an interim pastor she was even more suspicious and had basically decided take her chances with the position in New Mexico.

Interestingly enough, Ron Whiteside was not on the Search Committee, nor was he involved in anything official that was at work in the call that was extended to Rameeka. Rameeka wondered how Ron knew so much. Someone on the Search Committee had to be keeping Ron informed. Ron had an inflated opinion of himself, and felt in his heart and mind that he had "gotten Rameeka the position". Nothing could have been further from the truth. Rameeka didn't do backroom deals when it came to obtaining employment. If she wasn't hired into a position on her own merit she would not accept the position at all. Ron could have kept his secret phone calls and backhanded offers. He couldn't do anything for Rameeka except to be a good church member. In Rameeka's opinion, he couldn't even do that.

Ron Whiteside along with his friend Timothy had played a key role along with others behind the scenes with the removal of Rameeka from the position as Pastor of Holy Hill. He worked with them to keep the lies and innuendos moving so that the ugliness spread. In spite of it all, this was still a small group of people who were not in leadership but who wanted control at any price.

Sometimes anger and bitterness are expressed in actions that breed destruction. Rameeka guessed that Ron and Timothy must have held onto some anger and bitterness that preceded her. However, they took their frustration out upon Rameeka. They never considered that their failure to be elected to the offices they desired was the result of a vote for other candidates. Rameeka didn't stop the election nor did she enter into it; the people of Holy Hill spoke through their votes. They didn't elect Ron or Timothy.

Then there was Raymond Slater, lead singer of the "Aria" Choir. That choir was known by the youth of Holy Hill as the "Old People's Choir". The choir sang classical music, spirituals and other forms of 'high church' music. Under the leadership of an outstanding director, Evan Bachman, an excellent musician in his own right, the choir did well. This particular choir was angry with Rameeka for not paying enough attention to them in their minds. What they never understood was that Rameeka loved all music; she had even considered majoring in music when she was in college. She played the piano, had sung in a teen R and B group in high school, tried her hand at songwriting, and even sang in a couple of night clubs in Chicago years ago. The Aria Choir never took the time to listen to Rameeka's words when she addressed music. All music was sacred and important to her.

The Aria Choir had been at Holy Hill Church since its beginning. The members were stalwart in their achievements and in their time as members of the church. They felt they had paid their dues; they carried themselves as if the world owed them respect for their class and style. Sadly, their style was still forty years old and had ceased to develop beyond that time. Although the Director of the Aria Choir, Evan Bachman, was as supportive of Rameeka as anyone could have been, most of the twenty-five members didn't like Rameeka and never had. Rameeka just wasn't Hank, and her style wasn't like Hank's style. The Aria Choir members allowed Ray to influence them in ways that were destructive to the church. Ray Slater came over to shake hands with Rameeka.

"I am so sorry things didn't work out. I wish you well and I know you will be fine. You will find something else and you will move on. It just didn't—it just didn't work out. See, you and I didn't agree on some things, and I know that, but, uh, uh …."

Rameeka just froze her smile and looked directly into Ray's eyes. His gaze shifted away from Rameeka's eyes for the fourth time. Then he offended her completely. He said, "Aww, we still love you," as he took his rolled up church newsletter and smacked Rameeka on the left shoulder.

Rameeka said, "God bless you." God had nothing to do with what was on Rameeka's mind about Ray. Ray's wife couldn't look Rameeka in the face as she walked up to her. She just said, "I wish you the best, Rev." Rameeka's frozen smile didn't tell what was in her heart.

"God bless you," Rameeka said firmly. Ray's wife slithered away to find Ray who had moved to the other side of the narthex.

As she walked to her friend's car that last day at Holy Hill Church, Rameeka relived every moment of her experience with Holy Hill Church. She remembered everything from when she preached as a guest preacher for that call, to the first Sunday past the installation, to the first experience of the lies and innuendos.

In Rameeka's mind, the ugliness began many years before she came to Holy Hill. At least some of that ugliness was in the lives and experiences of the dissidents who never dealt with their own life issues. Most of the dissidents were troublemakers for Hank Hanley. The same people who were troublemakers during Rameeka's time at Holy Hill were also troublemakers when Hank Hanley was the pastor of Holy Hill.

They were involved in any negativity that came up; they even wrote anonymous letters to Hank just as they had done to Rameeka. They carried on quite badly and were always in the midst of controversy. Hank Hanley had led Holy Hill Church like the Pentecostal pastor that he was. He was in charge, he was the boss, and he led the church with an iron hand. Most of the members of Holy Hill were accustomed to that style. It was in their religious and denominational DNA. So was their resistance to female clergy.

Most of the members of Holy Hill Church came from families who migrated from southern and southwestern states such as Texas, Mississippi, Louisiana, Arkansas, and there were a few in the congregation from Mexico, Puerto Rico, Japan, Korea, and New Mexico. They were mostly African-Americans, although there were a few were Euro-Americans, and there were Native American Indians, Asians and Latinos. Holy Hill had always been multicultural; it reflected the Los Angeles culture of which it was a part.

Holy Hill was a church that welcomed people of all races, cultures, and lifestyles—after all, this was Los Angeles. There was visible representation of intermarriage, others who had not moved from the community, still others who chose to move into the community, and ultimately who had become members of Holy Hill. Rameeka enjoyed the mix of people and learned from everyone's history and culture.

One of her favorite annual church events was the Multicultural Ministry Fair. Everyone would prepare food from their native culture, wear their indigenous dress, and invite all the friends and family they could contact. There were games, childcare, special activities for the children and youth, and greetings from the mayor, city council person for their area, and a few others. On that day Holy Hill Church was the place to be and its members came out in full force. One would never know any dissension existed.

Most of the Holy Hill members came from modest, poor and some impoverished backgrounds. They had accomplished much in their lives and were solidly middle class, upper middle class, and some were even on the economic level of Aaron Morrow. That was rich by Holy Hill standards. It was rich by any standard, but the reality was that they still had scars on their souls. Some of those scars were the result of racial discrimination, an insensitive society, intolerance regarding immigration, and conflict they couldn't control. Some of the scars were the result of family issues coupled with the pain of a living and working in a society that still did not value African-Americans, other people of color, or their contributions.

For many African-Americans, the scars on the soul began before America's birth. The scars passed on for generations. The scars were in the making before those who withstood discrimination, racism, poverty and overwork had even been born. Scars on the soul implant themselves when we hear the stories of our fore-parents who survived the slave ships from Africa, the dehumanizing conditions Chinese people often faced upon arriving in the United States, the oppression of Native American Indians, the Japanese internment camps, the cruel treatment of Latino immigrants, and the poor treatment of the Irish, Italians, and others. Many of these brave people endured what many cannot envision so that others who came later could benefit.

Many who lived in centuries past as well as during the 20th century had withstood dehumanizing conditions and racism that would turn a person's stomach. The cruel treatment African people experienced from plantation owners, and equally difficult conditions at a freedom that only brought freedom in words were realities in so many families' lives and history. The stories provide some understanding of how many of our ancestors sacrificed and how they managed to leave a legacy in spite of it all for those of us who figuratively stand on their shoulders today.

Scars on the soul continued to take hold during the backlash to Reconstruction, during Jim Crow, during the Civil Rights Movement, and other events right up to the present day. The legacy of so many who fought for equality regardless of their race, including the "almost-would have been" success of Affirmative Action have left their mark on society. At some point the scars took root and implanted themselves in a fine pastor like Hank Hanley, causing him to take out his hurt and anger upon the white religious system in which he grew his ministry.

Rameeka could only imagine how many times Hank Hanley, his wife Amelia, and many others had been called the "N" word, relegated to the back cars on trains, back seats of busses, or treated badly by people and systems who felt it was their right to do so. Hank had endured discrimination beyond what many people can fathom as he grew up in Texas. He brought those unhealed scars from childhood to Los Angeles after college and seminary. He held mistrust for the white system, and he taught his members not to trust it. Hank projected his mistrust and hurt onto the region because of its lack of support for him, and because of the racist manner in which he was treated upon his entrée to Los Angeles. He taught the congregation not to have much contact with the region or the congregations in the region.

The scars on Hank's soul were firmly in place when he married his wife Amelia. Not knowing it, Hank proceeded to rule and oppress her, thinking he was just 'being the man of his household'. He remembered the cruel racism he endured in childhood, during his teen years, and when he traveled to Los Angeles to become the pastor of Holy Hill Independent Church. The district director at that time met him once, gave him the directions to the church, and told him there were no keys because of recent break-ins. Hank went to an empty church building in deep need of repair. He walked through a parsonage that was unlivable. He made up his mind that he would be successful at this new place no matter how hard he had to work. He called his wife Amelia, told her he would be awhile sending for her because he had to put things in order. He did just that. He went to work. He visited her whenever he could and sent for her at least twice a year for three years.

Eventually the parsonage was repaired and Hank could bring his family to Los Angeles. He made up his mind that he would build Holy Hill Church and lead it in a way that would not render him or his church dependent upon the district or regional office for anything.

Hank left a legacy that was unparalleled in many ways for the Los Angeles Area. In other ways Hank left a legacy that would be imitated by many other pastors and community organizers. The strength of that legacy achieved much for the people of Los Angeles and for the people of the world. Every legacy has a positive side and a less than positive side because these legacies are built by human beings who are part of human systems.

The other side of the story was that Hank carried the unhealed scars of racism with him throughout his life. They were scars on his soul. From Texas to Los Angeles racism was firmly planted in California Society.

Hank didn't let the reality of racism stop him from building God's Kingdom, but the pain in his heart, mind and soul never truly healed. He carried un-reconciled pain to his grave. One reason for the unhealed condition might be that our nation has never reconciled racism, discrimination, or its effect upon society as a whole. The country just continues to move on as if these atrocities have ended.

Hank's hurt never healed; it just spread. His illnesses, Parkinson's and mental illness were interpreted by some as a physical reflection of unresolved emotional and mental hurt. They were scars on his soul. Scars on the soul could give way to achievements in society, but those achievements did not heal Hank's soul. His energy for ministry, his never ending work for justice, his brilliant mind, and his voice that continually cried out for equality could not be stopped. His soul never healed and his heart never mended. The effects of the scars just implanted themselves more deeply into Hank's being. What he didn't discuss with anyone just kept getting buried deeper and deeper, and eventually Hank's behavior belied his real feelings.

During the first three years at Holy Hill Church Hank traveled home whenever he could, wrote to his wife, sent her money, and celebrated the birth of each of the five children they brought into the world. By the birth of their second child, the parsonage was finally repaired to livable conditions. Hank was able to travel back to Texas to retrieve his family. He could finally live with his family as God intended. His achievements continued along with his unresolved bitterness toward the denomination, the region, the district, and the whites in charge. They could do whatever they wanted at the regional office and around the region, but he was in charge of Holy Hill, his family, and his community. That's the way he rolled for the entire sixty years he pastored the church.

Hank was the man. His wife knew he was in charge, his children knew he was in charge, and his community knew he was in charge. He was in total control. Except for Rochelle, the psychiatrist he saw, and the hospital where he would be a patient for mental health issues and later for Parkinson's disease, he was always in total control. Somehow that control broke as Hank reached a point where he could no longer hide his illnesses.

It began with little things like losing his temper then pretending it never happened. He would hold the unsteady hand with the stronger, more solid hand until he dropped a glass of water one day. Then he began to say he had already had refreshments, or Rochelle would have someone bring the refreshments to the office and pretend that Hank was either on a conference call or in a meeting. The people on the receiving side were too ashamed to share the incidents with anyone so they never said anything until Hank had retired. The inability to face facts continued even when

Hank would become ill and not be able to stop his hands from shaking at all.

Later he was not able to keep his appointments. He would leave Rochelle to handle those things. It continued with his paranoia spiraling out of control, and Rochelle would find him curled up in a corner in his office thinking the lights were missiles that were coming toward him. Rochelle learned how to deal with him in ways his wife never could. She could talk to him, bring him up from the corner, get him to take his meds, and into the car to drive him to Dr. Wingfield. There was even an entrance to Wingfield's office the public didn't know. Dr. Wingfield made things easier for Hank; he respected and loved him but even though he would never become a member of the church for personal reasons, he took excellent care of Hank and kept Rochelle informed of everything. Hank was Dr. Wingfield's "Pastor".

Hank gave Dr. Wingfield permission for Rochelle to be the first to know everything. Then Hank would break the information to Amelia when we could; Rochelle had to take care of the details as Hank's condition worsened. Amelia was always the second person to know anything regarding Hank's situation. For years Hank thought he was protecting Amelia and his family by not worrying them with his illnesses. He didn't tell Amelia and he didn't tell his siblings. He just kept the painful secrets to himself and leaned on Rochelle. Eventually that was just the way things were. Hank never discussed anything, Amelia pretended everything was fine, and Rochelle suffered in silence.

Hank held a trust in Rochelle that no one could penetrate, especially not Amelia. Rochelle dealt with Hank's mistresses with professional courtesy and firm control. She even took secret child support to Selena, who had Hank's lovechild in Altadena. Selena never told anyone who the father was. She just pocketed the money, raised her son John, and as Hank's illness escalated to a crescendo, Selena took young John and quietly moved to Chicago one day. They never returned to California. Only Rochelle knew where they were or that they existed. Rochelle was the only one at the church besides Hank who knew about Selena Brown and young John Hanley Brown.

Hank continued to deteriorate physically and mentally. His illnesses were debilitating but during some of his lucid moments he talked with Rochelle. In those moments Hank realized what he had done and the difficulty he caused. He apologized for placing Rochelle into the middle of his issues. He said he was sorry. Hank had insisted that Rochelle keep all of his secrets, placing undue pressure upon her to take child support and other money to Altadena for little John Hanley Brown.

He told her how wrong it was to have had extramarital affairs. On one occasion Rochelle visited Hank in the hospital and listened to him talk incessantly about how wrong he had been to make such a mockery of his own personal life with having one affair after another. He asked

God's forgiveness and Rochelle's forgiveness. Then they prayed together. As Rochelle prayed with him and for him, she felt a burden lift from her heart. She was a forgiving person and she readily let Hank know that they would put the past behind them.

Rochelle had her own crosses to bear. She had actually allowed herself to be placed into those positions. She prayed for forgiveness to God, but she also told Hank that she should have and could have said "no". She remembered the last time they discussed the issues of Hank's infidelity and the ongoing string of affairs.

"You know, Hank, God is a forgiving God and loving God. When we ask forgiveness it is already done in the revelation of Jesus Christ. You preach that every chance you have. You have to believe it for yourself. Now, know that God forgives you, and you need to work hard to forgive yourself. No one is perfect, and all of us are sinners saved by grace. Concentrate on that and be grateful for it."

Hank smiled and said, "Who's the pastor around here?"

Rochelle said, "You are, but sometimes I am."

They laughed and held hands as a reconciled sister and brother in Christ. They were in good relationship, especially now, and could move forward with no more guilt, no more anger, and no more frustration.

Like her husband, but in different ways, scars on the soul of Amelia Hanley never healed. She became more and more aware that she would never be first in Hank's life. Holy Hill Church was his wife, his mistress, his love, and his life. Their five children couldn't even reach a top place in Hank's heart. Hank had a secret life Amelia could never know or enter. His work took precedent over everything. She thought about all of the arguments as a result of his life in ministry and the lack of life with the family. Hank was never really engaged in family life. His life was Holy Hill Church, the surrounding community, and the Greater Los Angeles Area. His life was anywhere Amelia was not. Amelia's life was Hank and their children. Even during her affairs she could not be satisfied; she just wanted to matter to Hank. In Amelia's mind, she never seemed to matter to Hank.

Amelia became embittered to the point that she refused any help at all when Hank became unable to care for himself. She refused help from members, she refused the daily nursing care service, which they could well afford, and she refused help from family. She insisted on handling everything for Hank all by herself. She could not. She kept trying, but Hank was 6'4" and weighed 235 lbs. She couldn't lift him, feed him, or encourage him to take his meds.

During the last nine months of Hank's life the illnesses took their toll. When Amelia brought him to church there were times when Hank didn't even know where he was. He had an odor, his appearance was disshelved, his feet were swollen quite badly, and he would mumble incoherently. The members would see him, speak to him, and walk away in tears because the giant they knew and loved had been reduced to a sick, ill-kept man who didn't know his name let alone theirs, and he could no longer function. Eventually Hank deteriorated to a sad and broken place.

Scars on the soul of the old women who hated Rameeka were most likely reflective of their own oppression from earlier years at least that was how Rameeka saw things. Most of these women were more than seventy-five years old; they came from Southern States like Louisiana, Arkansas, and Mississippi. Rameeka could only speculate at the oppressive society in which they grew up. Segregation was the order of the day and racism was seen as a privilege and a regular everyday experience. Rameeka could only guess at the level of rape, molestation, violence, verbal cruelty and hatred they had experienced during their formative and teen years.

When Ross Andrew Wayne's case went to court and Aaron Morrow was later sent to prison for fifteen years, Rameeka remembered it was Amelia and her circle of elderly ladies who gossiped about Ross, who trashed him to others, and who treated him badly. In their minds, Ross was a wayward young boy who had seduced a kindly older man. The elderly women loved Aaron for his looks, his wealth, his persona, and his charisma no matter what he had done. He was always one who gave a meaningless compliment with finesse and grandness.

Aaron may have represented what was missing in their own lives, so the lonely, elderly single women made him something opposite of what he was, which was a child predator. When Ross Wayne left Holy Hill Church and moved to Germany to further his studies in music, none of the elderly ladies made mention of it. The men hosted a special dinner and concert to encourage him. They provided him with a scholarship as well. One anonymous donor paid for Ross to obtain counseling.

Many of the men of the Holy Hill Church were very angry with Aaron. They shunned him; then they banned together to see that he was removed from church offices he held, especially the Men's Ministry Group. Several of them approached him and asked how he could do something like molesting and raping young boys. Aaron denied everything right up to the trial. After numerous denials and attempts to plead with far lesser charges, Aaron finally pleaded guilty to thirty-six counts of various acts of rape of a minor and was sentenced to twenty-five years in prison.

Aaron's support came from the women of the church like Amelia and others, who visited Aaron Morrow in jail and in prison, wrote letters to him, and who kept his name alive within the church. They catered to his wife; they comforted her and pledged their loyalty to Aaron. Rameeka suspected that these women may have been abused themselves and never received any help. Their behavior belied their life experiences in Rameeka's estimation. In order to be so cruel toward a child who had been raped and molested, Rameeka felt that Amelia and her friends had to have been abused and oppressed. All she could do was to pray for them. Only God in Christ Jesus could heal scars on their souls.

Scars on the soul of Holy Hill Church couldn't heal as long as the secrets were kept undercover and as long as people were in denial. Church growth and professionals of healthy functioning churches have written about these issues for several years. Only a wound that is treated and exposed to a healing balm, medical attention, cleanliness, and fresh air can really heal. The deeper the wounds and scars the more treatment is needed. Many of the Holy Hill members didn't know they needed healing, treatment, prayer, and consolation. They turned their anger at the exposure of their ills upon their current pastor, Pastor Rameeka.

In the minds of the dissidents, Rameeka had aired the church's dirty laundry, uncovered its secrets, and she had stuck her nose where it didn't belong. In the minds of the dissenters Rameeka was at fault. She had created the problems Holy Hill had experienced.

Eventually the elderly women like Amelia and her friends began to meet secretly together, recruit others to meet with them, and to share all they didn't like about Rameeka. One of their dislikes was when Rameeka brought a new way of celebrating worship and Holy Communion. They didn't like that she brought office hours to Holy Hill Church. They didn't like that the board agreed, approved, and saw to it that those hours were enforced. Hank never imposed office hours on the congregation. He was always at the Church and always had an open door policy. Hank lived five houses from the Church, and walked there by 7:30 a.m. daily. Sometimes he didn't go home until midnight.

Those who disliked Rameeka didn't care that she lived in Pasadena, drove to the office by 9:30 a.m., sometimes went to lunch, and threatened to go home about 6:00 p.m. except for board meeting days, special events, and choir rehearsal days. Of course the elderly ladies didn't care that she went to the hospital after she left the church, and that she often remained there until 10:00 p.m. whenever there was a need. There were many times she would meet families at the hospital at 7:00 a.m. then continue to Holy Hill afterward.

When a group doesn't like or appreciate a pastor, it doesn't matter how hard the pastor serves. Nothing satisfies them. That was the story of the dissidents. Nothing satisfied them. Rameeka wasn't Hank, and even though Hank was dead and some of them didn't like him, he was still alive in the minds of certain people. Rameeka wondered if they wanted to bring him back to life. She wondered if Amelia and her friends wanted to resurrect Hank. They certainly tried.

Truthfully thinking, in Rameeka's mind Amelia took an immediate dislike to Rameeka, and she was hostile from day one. That was the truth and many members noticed it. Rameeka was always polite and respectful to Amelia, but Rameeka's respect for Amelia and her commitment to Amelia as a member and as a woman who had special needs went unheeded and often unrecognized by

Amelia and her friends. When the dissident group began meeting secretly, Rameeka knew something sinister was happening she just didn't know what it was. Eventually the dissidents sent complaint letters to the district and even the regional office, but Rameeka had already activated her search for another position. She began connecting with her colleagues in other areas and who were in positions to help her receive another position. After five years at Holy Hill it was time. Her actions just didn't happen quickly enough.

At one point in the process Rameeka requested a special task force to come to Holy Hill and to investigate. That was a process that was available to congregations that were in conflict. She requested that task force from the district and the regional offices. She provided information to the offices that would have resulted in a special program to help the congregation to work through its difficulties. She had done those programs herself with other churches and most were successful. The offices never responded to her requests. Her requests for assistance within the region went unheeded.

The dissidents accused Rameeka of many atrocities that baffled her mind. They accused her of embezzlement, fraud, and financial malfeasance to the tune of $60,000. Later, their stories increased the amount to $350,000. If that wasn't enough, the dissidents accused Rameeka of trying to take Amelia's home away from her. They believed the home Hank eventually bought was officially a parsonage. They also accused Rameeka of taking kickbacks from the building repair project and changing too much too soon. They printed slanderous brochures and distributed them to the congregation and all over the community. Then they wrote letters and signed petitions that they sent to the district and regional offices.

The letters went to the district and regional offices without any notice to Rameeka or to the church board. Amelia and her friends signed the letters and recruited others to do the same. The letters were signed by community residents who were not members, several youth under eighteen from Holy Hill, the lead dissident members, and anyone else the group could convince. They took their best shot and still had the support and signatures of only about fifteen to twenty percent of the total Sunday attendance. Usually the number of Sunday morning participants was about 450. The total church membership was now 550.

The district director and one associate director contacted the national office about the Holy Hill disaster. The office recommended a special independent parish consultant to work with Holy Hill. The national office of the denomination of which Holy Hill Church belonged recognized the independence of its congregations, but provided resources to help when requested or when a situation in a congregation was deemed beyond help. That was interpreted as the case of Holy Hill Church. The independent parish consultant program had been developed several years ago. The national office kept a bank of parish consultant resources— usually comprised of women and men who had built up a business and who were adept at this work. The parish consultant that was decided upon for Holy Hill was in business for himself, accomplished and had worked with large businesses and many non-profit organizations. He had years of broad based experience in these arenas. The problem Rameeka had with the process was that the consultant, Dr. Raymond Sizemore, had never served as a pastor and was not a professional within the same or similar faith as Holy Hill Church. There were definite theological differences between Rameeka's church and Ray Sizemore's church. He belonged to a charismatic faith that did not ordain women, had very fundamentalist positions about women, and was not likely to change. Ray had born into his particular faith, had continued to embrace it, and felt that his denominational affiliation did not interfere with his work as a parish consultant. Ray's work required open-mindedness and working closely with congregations that may have held very different beliefs from his. He felt that he embraced women in pastoral leadership and would never knowingly do anything to be non-supportive. Key word—"knowingly".

Dr. Sizemore had never been ordained and had never been a pastor. He was, however, committed to his faith and the church. Truly Ray attempted to be open-minded and worked hard to be fair. He was a fine established consultant within his own right. He was a seminary trained Ph.D. who also had a Ph.D. in business and finance. He stated that he had considered pastoral ministry, but decided he could serve the wider church more effectively and certainly make more money as a consultant. Financially Dr. Sizemore had done quite well. He was a good man who had a beautiful wife and six children; he was a very smart man and Rameeka really liked him, but in Rameeka's mind he was not the person to facilitate this church's process.

Rameeka felt that someone who had served as a pastor at some point, and someone who was also a pastor within the same denomination as Holy Hill would be more effective in the process. The reason, at least in Rameeka's mind, was because that person would have more in-depth understanding of the particularities of a church like Holy Hill. That person would understand the nuances of a denomination like that to which Rameeka belonged. However, in spite of her attention to this issue, Rameeka did not feel that her voice was heard or acknowledged. She had served this congregation for five years and felt that she had walked the faith journey with the people. She understood the unresolved grief, the hidden anger toward Hank, the need to cover up faults and only show the best side to the public. Rameeka understood the background of the elderly membership, the sacrifices they made to achieve, and the life experiences they would never share. A person within the same faith who had served as a pastor at some point in his or her career would have understood much more. Of course those were Rameeka's thoughts and feelings. However, they had merit because Rameeka had background education and experience in working with congregations in conflict and trauma as well as those on the parish consultant list.

Rameeka had voiced her concern, shared several names of pastors and denominational professionals who were in the bank of parish consultants with the national office and who would have done a fine job facilitating a conflict management program. However, Rameeka felt that her requests were ignored by the district and regional offices. The regional office made a decision that many felt hastened the "end" of Holy Hill Church.

Often small, hostile groups within a congregation will stop at nothing to rid a congregation of a pastor. They will fabricate stories, exaggerate the situation, lie about everything, and escalate the pressure of a situation to get what they want. If the church is destroyed in the process, then that is one consequence of the plan as a whole. In these cases the detractors don't always know what they are fighting. They may focus upon the new pastor or whatever the presenting issue seems to be. However, the deeper issues are overlooked or glossed over because the focus is so intent. The detractors of Holy Hill Church were focused upon Rameeka and never looked any deeper into the real issues.

The dissenters of Holy Hill Church took a 'no holds barred' approach to assure Rameeka's departure. The group not only wanted her to leave, but it wanted to destroy Rameeka's reputation, her professional stance, and her entire career. Rameeka never knew the real reason why the group was so hostile, but at least she felt that she knew the anonymous letters she had received for the entire five years came from certain members of the dissident group and from certain people of the Aria Choir. She knew that the internet fabrications were written by Janice Devereaux, a lifetime member of Holy Hill.

Rameeka received that at least three anonymous letters came from Janice Devereaux. Of the many anonymous letters that came to her over the five years, Rameeka was convinced that some came from Janice and her accomplice Leslie. The letters were typewritten on a computer, but the envelopes were handwritten, so when Rameeka compared the handwriting on the envelopes the writing was the same. Rameeka prayed for Janice, who had been diagnosed as bipolar, developmentally challenged, and morbidly obese. Her mother died when Janice was 8; her father raised her. He never remarried.

It was Janice Devereaux who called several members of Holy Hill to tell them that she knew all along that Aaron Morrow had been molesting Ross Wayne. Janice's daughter was in the same class with Ross in junior high and high school. She saw Aaron and Ross together on numerous occasions. Janice's daughter reported that she had witnessed Aaron touching Ross on certain occasions when Aaron thought no one noticed. However, she was afraid to say anything except to Janice. Janice felt important with the knowledge that she knew and shared about Ross and Aaron. She felt that she knew information that others did not know; it made her feel superior in some way because she had knowledge of something that others did not possess. Rameeka thought that perhaps Janice's self-esteem was enmeshed in being able to provide something of which others were unaware.

Janice was sixty years of age, lived in a small house on her father's property, and never moved from her father's control. At some point in her life she had given birth to two daughters, both of whom were diagnosed with the same illnesses as their mother. All three members of the Devereaux Family, Janice and her daughters, Sage and Summer, were morbidly obese. Each was 5'10" and easily weighed 400 lbs. Rumors of incest between Mr. Devereaux, Janice, Sage, and Summer abounded among the members of Holy Hill Church. However, no formal complaint ever took place nor did anyone ever talk with the women themselves. In addition if questioned the gossipers would deny ever having made a statement. It was yet another buried secret of Holy Hill Church. People talked about others but not with them. People would not address issues directly, they wrote anonymous letters, gossiped among themselves, and walked around with buried secrets and unhealed scars on their souls. This behavior had taken place for a number of years, beginning during Hank's service as pastor. It was never addressed or corrected.

These actions were the marks of a truly unhealthy congregation. In these situations people thrived on secrets, lies and innuendos. They didn't confront those with whom there was an issue; they told everyone else about it. The thought was that the message would get back to the person/people with whom there was an issue. The trouble was that the stories were usually exaggerated and blown way up by the time the "message" got back to the source. Rameeka began to wonder when the unhealthy process that was so entrenched at Holy Hill might have taken place. It happened long before Rameeka came to Holy Hill. It was something in the center and in the "soul" of Holy Hill, where it began would always be a question. How it continued would always be a mark of shame. When it would cease was an ongoing work of healing.

During the consultation process with Dr. Sizemore, Rameeka took the initiative to leave Holy Hill. It seemed the only productive thing to do. Rameeka had given all she could give. The detractors would not calm down, nor would they ever. Dr. Sizemore had suggested that Rameeka should take a leave of absence and then return to Holy Hill. However, if she took "leave" and returned, what would be different? The troublemakers would merely have some months to aggressively place themselves into positions of power or into positions in which they could continue to manipulate. She believed the difficulties would never go away, and that there would be an ongoing fight that would not cease.

Why should she continue to work hard to bring health to a place that resisted and fought it at every hand? Therefore, prior to the consultant's final report Rameeka explained her decision. In her mind there was no turning back, and even though she later rethought her decision, she still came out with the same idea. It was time to end this phase of her ministry with this particular congregation.

Rameeka's father was a U.S. Army veteran. He used to speak wise words of wisdom to her in language that she often had to think about so that those words really made an impact. Once he told her, "Baby, know when to advance, know when to retreat, and know when to stand your ground." He would have said that and more to her at this time. His words came to mind as she thought about Holy Hill and the experience. "Know when to hold 'em and know when to fold 'em." It was time to fold and to let go. It was time to look at where God was leading her next.

Part of her decision revolved around the importance of reaching and enjoying physical, spiritual, emotional, and mental well-being. It was important to achieve and maintain a good balance in life, and that was lacking with the Holy Hill Church these days. She felt that with the ugliness of the situation, the high level of conflict, and the health issues it had begun to cause her, remaining as the pastor was not worth the fight. Somebody had to be healthy, and if Holy Hill didn't want to be healthy, Rameeka did.

Rameeka wanted to live and enjoy life. Her five years at Holy Hill Church had become a serious nightmare. Maybe God's work for Rameeka at Holy Hill had been accomplished. She had truly worked hard, long, and had given of herself in so many ways. Rameeka felt that she had given far more than she had ever received. Maybe she only felt that way for the moment because the reality of what had occurred was so fresh. The work for Holy Hill had not been finished, and there were still mountains to overcome. There always would be; the church was made up of sinful human beings who were created by a Lord who had no sin.

Well, they were all just human beings trying to get through life as painlessly as possible. Sometimes the road to eternity was paved with one obstacle after another. When a person overcame one difficult situation, another was waiting to rear its head. There would always be situations as long the world and the church were comprised of human beings. We were all just imperfect people who had the blessed fortune to be created by a perfect God.

That particular God, that perfect God, that omnipresent God gave, lent, or sent (in Greek the word could mean any of the three) God's only Begotten Son for the benefit of all human beings. When Rameeka thought about that reality she found joy in the midst of all the deep conflict and heartbreak she was experiencing at that time.

A wise and lovely lady once told Rameeka, "My Dear, the church is a microcosm of society. You will always find the same societal ills right here in the church. We don't leave our sickness and perversions at the door when we attend worship or when we serve. We bring our baggage with us. That's why we are here." Elleene Kingsley, a retired church leader, shared those words of wisdom when Rameeka was in a tough place years ago.

After that visit with Elleene, Rameeka went home, prayed, meditated, and walked into her office the next morning with a smile and an agenda for that particular congregation. That was twenty-five years earlier when Rameeka was serving her very first congregation. Rameeka would always remember Elleene; she was thoughtful, kind, and very direct. She shared her heart and soul with Rameeka and with those who took the time to talk with her. Now Elleene was part of the great cloud of witnesses who were preparing heaven for the rest of humanity.

Rameeka would not allow the Holy Hill Church experience to destroy her physical health, her spiritual well-being, or her mental and emotional health. She would leave before she would be destroyed. Raymond and the regional staff respected her decision. Rameeka would leave with scars on her soul, but the Lord of the soul would be present with her through the power of the Holy Spirit to assure her healing. Rameeka committed herself to healing and to healing well.

Rameeka wanted the scars on her soul to heal. During the twelve months' severance from Holy Hill Church Rameeka exercised, stepped up her reading, sought a counselor to help her process the pain, wrote memoirs, and prepared herself for the next call. All she could do was ask God to remain with her in the search, to stay with her during this part of the faith journey. She prayed that God would allow her to be victorious on the other side.

As the months continued Rameeka read fine books, worked through the counseling, and continued to exercise. She took on several projects at home and completed some additional projects that she might never have completed. The year was a good one, and Rameeka took every advantage of it.

One day Rameeka answered her telephone. A man's deep voice was on the other end. "Good morning. I would like to speak with Rev. Rameeka Middlebrooks."

"Yes, this is Rev. Middlebrooks. How may I help you?"

"Rev., my name is Vernon Benson Charles. I am the chair of the search committee for Faith Independent Church in Newport Beach. Your resume has been sent to me, and I would like to know if you are interested in considering our congregation to be our senior pastor."

"Thank you for your call, sir. I would certainly be interested. Where in Newport Beach are you located?"

Well, God was still working by God's spirit. Rameeka had some hope and some considerations. Rameeka and Mr. Charles completed their conversation and made some preliminary arrangements. Rameeka prayed for God's guidance and God's leading in this possibility. "Dear Lord, allow your will to be done and to reflect your glory. In Jesus' Name I pray, Amen."

Rameeka reflected upon the last nine months or so in which she had been at rest, in discernment, and in personal growth about what had and what was going to happen. She had learned so much about herself, her leadership, and her commitment to God's call. She learned how she would structure the next ministry, how she would conduct the educational sessions with the church boards, church officers, and how she would plan church programs. Rameeka would allow God to guide her and lead her in whatever the next call would be. In other words, Rameeka would be open to whatever God's call for her would be and wherever it would lead.

Holy Hill Church was struggling to rebuild and to move forward following the events of the past year. The strong leaders of Holy Hill Church were devastated at the accusations, the slanderous brochures, and the petitions that just seemed to have appeared. The church board, officers and the strong majority of members of Holy Hill loved their pastor, appreciated her, and wanted her to remain at the church for the remainder of her career. When the stories about secret meetings circulated along with the brochures, the supporters did not know what to do. They thought the conflict would go away; they really felt that the situation was just a bump in the road and that it would all just work itself out. It didn't work out the way so many of them hoped.

Holy Hill would never be the same. Holy Hill Church had to live in the aftermath of an exodus of almost half its membership, including most of the strong, vital church officers who were serving actively at that time. The strong leaders left Holy Hill and eventually joined other churches; they became officers of their new congregations. The former dissidents of Holy Hill Church worked themselves into becoming church officers. Holy Hill Church searched for a new pastor, but the word was out in the church world. No pastor wanted to lead a congregation that had spent so much time, energy, and effort to oust an honest, caring pastor who really was already seeking a new position. The search was long and hard. It was so hard that the next pastor who followed Rameeka found challenges he had not expected. All Rameeka could do was to pray for Holy Hill Church, its people, and its future. She wanted the church to have one; she didn't know how it would without a strong program of transformation. That was no longer Rameeka's issue; she had long since let go and had moved into another phase of life in Christ Jesus. That phase would be her best ministry yet.

Rameeka called Rochelle. "Hi Rochelle. What are you doing?"

"Not much today. I cleaned and organized some things here at the apartment. Are you all right? I've been quite worried about you."

"I'm okay. Got scars on my soul, but I will be fine. Keeping in prayer, taking on new projects here at home and doing a new resume for a position I might consider. Have you been to Texas yet?"

"Not yet. Maybe next month. I am planning to fly to Austin with Janie, Jeannie, Jeri, and Johnnie for a week then we will travel over to Dallas to see Janet." Janet was Rochelle's sister. Janet had moved to Lubbock, Texas with her daughter, Kelly, and her son-in-law Cole. They were expecting their first child, and Rochelle was excited about becoming a great aunt for the first time. Rochelle and her children were very close. They enjoyed traveling together, spending holidays and special times together. The five of them had always enjoyed spending time together.

"I'm so glad you are going to Texas and that all of you will be together. So, we need to get together before then. How about sushi and sake this evening? My treat. Can you go?"

Rochelle shouted joyfully, "ABSOLUTELY!!! What time? I'll meet you at our favorite place."

The scars on Rameeka's soul would continue to heal with God's help; in fact, the healing was progressing quite well. She would continue to seek a new position and would hold on to her faith in the process. God was faithful and knew what she was experiencing. God would guide, lead, and care for all God's people, Holy Hill and Rameeka included. Holding on to that reality would take Rameeka through her last several months into a new reality.

Sometimes Rameeka wondered how Holy Hill Church Independent Church would fare in the aftermath of the deep conflict. So many members had left, joined other congregations, and had made new congregational affiliations. Others had not removed their names from the church rolls, but had not returned and vowed never to do so. All of the effort to remove Rameeka from the pastoral office had taken a hard and painful toll on the church and upon everyone connected to it. Those members who remained worked hard to forget the past; however, until one faces the difficulty and owns his or her part in it true reconciliation cannot take place. At this point in time Holy Hill Church would work to find a new pastor, and hope to recover in some way. In the meantime, Rameeka would meet with the search committee in Newport Beach and look with expectant hope and anticipation for a new future. That would be God's gift to her and would bring further healing for the scars on her own soul.

CPSIA information can be obtained
at www.ICGtesting.com
Printed in the USA
LVHW080158100619
620680LV00021B/334/P